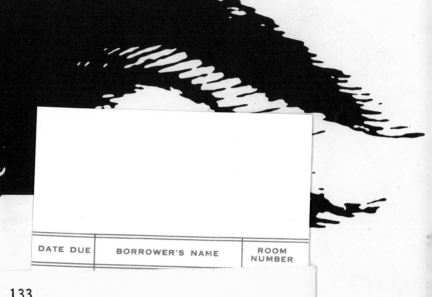

RUDLEY, STEPHEN

Psychic detectives

GRAPHIC DESIGN BY NICHOLAS KRENITSKY

STEPHEN RUDLEY

PSYCHIC DETECTIVES

FRANKLIN WATTS

NEW YORK | LONDON

1979

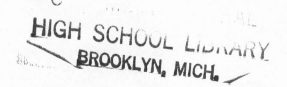

TO Cynthia AND Slugger,
AND ESPECIALLY Annie

Library of Congress Cataloging in Publication Data

Rudley, Stephen.
    Psychic detectives.

    Bibliography: p.
    Includes index.
    SUMMARY: Explores extrasensory abilities,
traces their role in other times and cultures, and in-
vestigates cases involving psychic detectives.
    1. Parapsychology and criminal investigation—
Juvenile literature. [1. Parapsychology and crimi-
nal investigation. 2. Criminal investigation] I.
Title.
BF1045.C7R83   364.12'8   78-23939
ISBN 0-531-02928-X

CONTENTS

INTRODUCTION

UNLIKE MORE CONVENTIONAL POLICE INVESTIGA-
tors, psychic detectives do not rely upon footwork, in-
terrogation, logical deduction, or intuition. Instead,
psychic detectives (both men and women) use their
talents of extrasensory perception to unravel the mysteries of crime.

IS IT REALLY POSSIBLE TO HELP SOLVE A CRIME SIM-
ply by holding a photograph of the victim? Is it really
possible to stand in a room where a murder has been
committed and receive visions of the killer at work?
Is it really possible to receive visions of a crime that
has not yet taken place? The answer to these questions is yes, if you happen to be a psychic detective.

vii

If you or I were allowed to visit the scene of a crime and handle, say, a scarf belonging to a kidnap victim, we probably wouldn't be able to learn anything about the crime except that the victim liked green silk scarves. Perhaps we might be able to detect a faint odor of perfume on the scarf; possibly we could identify the brand. But we wouldn't be able to provide even the most general description of the victim in question. Nor would we be able to determine who abducted her, nor why she was abducted, nor where she was being held.

In order to determine these facts we would have to search for witnesses, question family and friends of the victim, try to establish motives, a reason; and, of course, we would search the scene of the crime for physical clues: bits of hair, blood, paint, fibers, and other foreign matter that could have belonged to the kidnappers. Perhaps a gun was fired, perhaps a bullet will be uncovered, perhaps heel prints will be discovered and casts made.

In short, like Sherlock Holmes with his magnifying glass and astute powers of deduction, we would have to rely on clues recognizable by our senses and our powers of intellect.

What makes psychic deduction so important is that it relies on a completely new channel of perception to obtain information about crimes. The extra in extrasensory perception means beyond—beyond the five common senses. Psychic detectives perceive events in the world unbounded by the usual limitations of space and time. They appear to be able to tap information about past, present, and future, become aware of events beyond the range of the common senses, and tune into the mental processes of other people. As a result, people with psychic abilities provide police with a unique crimefighting tool.

A psychic detective handling the same green silk scarf at the scene of our imaginary kidnapping might well be able to provide a description of the kidnappers, their car, and their hideout—information that, if not an instant wrap-up of the case, could at least direct more conventional investigative efforts in the most productive ways.

IN THIS BOOK WE SHALL FIRST EXPLORE THE EXTRA-sensory abilities used by psychic detectives. Then we shall examine the scientists' views on psychic phenomena. Next we shall trace the role of psychic abilities through other times and cultures. Finally we shall investigate cases involving psychic detectives and delve into the nature of their relationship with the police.

To begin with we must answer a question or two. What are psychic abilities? What is ESP? What is *psychic* about psychic detectives? Let's take a look.

ESP?

WE ARE ALL FAMILIAR WITH THE SO-CALLED FIVE ordinary senses of sight, sound, taste, touch, and smell. (There are other ordinary senses as well: we also respond to pain, pressure, heat, cold, gravity, and a host of other internal sensations which we are never even aware of consciously.) These ordinary senses are the means by which we receive most of our information about the world around us, and in turn, communicate with it.

But these ordinary senses do not account for *all* the information we receive from our environment. Sometimes we learn about events that have taken place too far away to have been seen or heard, or we learn about them in a manner that can't be explained by normal senses. At other times we may become

3

aware of someone else's thoughts without being told or without receiving any sensory messages. Sometimes we may even receive information about events that have not yet happened. These cases cannot be accounted for by our ordinary senses. Instead, we explain them as resulting from extrasensory, or psychic, perceptions.

Our own society has been very slow to accept the evidence of psychic phenomena. But the evidence is there, it is strong, and there is much of it in hundreds of books, countless scientific papers, and thousands of cases and experiments. Indeed, an entire science, parapsychology, has come into being to study the phenomena.

In this chapter we shall explore telepathy, clairvoyance, and precognition, the three main types of ESP relied on by psychic detectives. (There are others, including psychokinesis, which is the ability of mind to affect matter by moving or bending objects through mental processes alone.)

Telepathy is the ability to become aware of the mental state of another person: to know what the person is thinking and/or feeling. *Clairvoyance* is the ability to perceive events that are impossible to perceive by the normal senses. Clairvoyance can operate at close range (the subject describes an object in a sealed box right in front of him) or at great distances (the subject perceives events taking place at distant target areas). *Precognition* is the ability to perceive future events. In all three phenomena (clairvoyance, telepathy, and precognition) information about the world reaches the perceiver through extrasensory

4

channels; the five common senses are not utilized. Telepathy, clairvoyance, and precognition are, therefore, all examples of extrasensory perception, or ESP.

HAVE YOU EVER HAD A PSYCHIC EXPERIENCE? WHEN asked, most of us search our memories for an unusually dramatic or catastrophic event: a plane we "knew" was going to crash, a relative whose unexpected death was already revealed to us in a dream, or a president whose assassination was witnessed in a waking vision.

Not all psychic events are of this nature. Perhaps the following example from the notes of Dr. Berthold Schwartz will seem more familiar to you. Dr. Schwartz conducted a ten-year study of his own family in which he recorded 1,500 incidents that he considered to be psychic. He published his results in a book entitled *Parent-Child Telepathy*.

December 20, 1961, Wednesday, 3:10 P.M. My intention of writing "First Class Mail" on an important letter . . . was completely frustrated because there was no red pen on my desk. My search for it was to no avail. My thoughts went, "Oh, I suppose Ardis [Dr. Schwartz's wife] took it for the Christmas cards and never returned it! That poor blue pen is no good." At that point Eric bounded downstairs and into my office. "Here, Daddy, is the red pen!" He [Eric] is quick to comply with a wish of his parents, *even when he is separated by distance, with no usual method of communication.* (italics mine)

5

Was this really a psychic event? Did Eric "read" his father's mind? Could it have been a coincidence instead? This is a problem in psychic research. The above example *could* have been due to coincidence. On the other hand, when one encounters such incidents time and time again, one begins to wonder if there isn't some other explanation—a psychic explanation.

Dr. Schwartz believes that psychic exchanges occur normally between people who are closely attached emotionally, as between the members of a family. He goes on to say that psychic events of this nature probably occur more frequently than most of us realize. The problem is that we do not usually recognize them for what they are because they are so very, very ordinary. They are easily dismissed as being mere coincidence or good guesswork.

NORMALLY OUR DREAMS, THOUGHTS, AND FANTASIES remain within the confines of our own consciousness. No one else knows what we are thinking about—normally.

A young Peruvian, Manuel Córdova-Rios, was kidnapped in the Amazon forest by Amahuaca Indians. During his captivity he took part in an ancient tribal ritual, one which demonstrated that normal experience is only half the story.

In a hidden clearing of a nearby forest, Manuel and his captors began to sing "magical" chants and perform special rituals that succeeded in developing a great feeling of closeness among the men in the group.

Then each man sipped an herbal drink called *aya-huasca*. Soon after they began to see visions.

At one point during the ritual, a memory was triggered in Manuel's mind. He remembered coming face to face with a rare black jaguar on an isolated jungle path. The very moment he thought about *his* black jaguar, a shudder traveled through the group; the others were seeing it too!

In *Wizard of the Upper Amazon,* Manuel Córdova-Rios explains that everyone in the group knew that the black jaguar vision had come from him. Somehow, without communicating in any ordinary way, eleven other people were able to "see" what one man was thinking. In fact, they were so impressed with the vision that they named Manuel Córdova-Rios Ino Moxo—black panther.

The two incidents just described are examples of telepathy. In the early days of parapsychology research, telepathy was considered to be a kind of mind-to-mind communication in which one person, the "sender," concentrated on a thought and "sent" it to the mind of a second person, the "receiver," in much the same way a radio picks up the signal sent by a broadcasting station.

During the 1930s psychical research amassed evidence making it clear that the "mental radio" picture was not very accurate. Experiments at Duke University conducted by J. B. Rhine demonstrated that it was *not* necessary for the person sending the message to be aware of his thought: unconscious thoughts could be picked up as well.

At present no one can really explain telepathy.

We still do not know exactly what it is or how it works. All we can say is that by some as yet unknown process, one person can become aware of what is going on inside the mind of another.

IN FRANCE IN THE LATE NINETEENTH CENTURY DR. Charles Richet performed experiments which suggested that a second kind of psychic phenomenon was at work. He found that some people could draw a picture that matched an unseen one in a sealed envelope. This could not be telepathy because only *one* person was involved. He called it a "sixth sense." Later card-guessing experiments designed by J. B. Rhine in the 1920s confirmed the existence of the new phenomenon, which we now call clairvoyance.

In *Psychic Children,* Samuel Young relates the following incident concerning a young girl named Jenny.

One day Jenny was playing Scrabble with her father. She beat him . . . again and again. He could not understand how his little daughter could keep drawing all the high scoring seven letter words she needed. When he asked her how she did it, she replied that it was simple. She just picked the letters she wanted.

"Listen," her father said, "I have four letters in my hand now. If I drew the right three I would have a seven letter word." He then told her he needed an M, B, and E. "I was so scared. If I could make *him* believe, I could make *anybody* believe . . . I closed my eyes and said a prayer and put my hand in the bag and pulled out the letters M, B, and E. He kind of screamed . . . 'O.K., she's got ESP!' "

BETWEEN 1956 AND 1959, PSYCHIC DETECTIVE Peter Hurkos took part in a series of experiments with neurologist-parapsychologist Andrija Puharich that were designed to further explore the phenomenon of clairvoyance. Before several witnesses Hurkos was given a sealed cardboard box. His task was to describe the object inside it. Hurkos's impressions were recorded by Puharich in his book *Beyond Telepathy*:

> This object blew up—an explosion. There was an explosion—a long time ago. I hear a strange language. It is very old. It had also to do with water. I don't know what it is. I see a dark color. It is not straight. Not regular. It is very jagged, sharp points. It belonged to three people. I am sure of this. Dr. Ducasse didn't buy this. It was given to him and it was repaired. A souvenir. I am sure the owner of the cylinder is dead. I do not mean Dr. Ducasse, he is well.

Hurkos couldn't say exactly what the object was. The Dr. Ducasse that Hurkos spoke about was the man who sent the sealed package for the experiment. He was not there when it took place. Only after the experiment was completed did he send a letter to Puharich explaining exactly what the object was and where it had come from. It was a small pottery jar given to him as a gift thirty-six years before by a friend who was now dead. The jar had come from the ruins of Pompeii, the Roman city that had been bur-

9

ied in an avalanche of lava from an eruption of Mount Vesuvius in A.D. 79.

ANOTHER TYPE OF CLAIRVOYANCE HAS BEEN STUDied in California at the Stanford Research Center. Russell Targ and Harold Puthoff performed experiments with what they called "remote viewing" and published their findings in their book *Mind Reach*.

In remote viewing, a subject is able to "see" a target that is impossible to see by ordinary means. The following test run was performed by noted psychic Ingo Swann.

A set of navigational coordinates—latitude and longitude, in degrees, minutes, and seconds—was presented to Mr. Swann. Could he clairvoyantly describe where and what these coordinates were?

The psychic closed his eyes and immediately began to report his visions. Occasionally he would open them to sketch a map. He described mounds or rolling hills, a city to the north, taller buildings, and smog. "This seems to be a strange place, somewhat like the lawns that one would find around a military base." He went on to describe what appeared to be underground bunkers or possibly a covered reservoir.

Then he came in for a closer view. He saw cliffs to the east, a fence to the north, a circular building —perhaps a tower. "Is this a former Nike [missile] base or something like that?" When he was finished he handed over his map. "This is about as far as I can go without feedback, and perhaps guidance as to what is wanted . . ."

A few weeks later they received a phone call from the skeptical colleague who had provided the target coordinates. Mr. Swann's description was correct in every detail, even as far as having the relative distances between points on his map in scale.

SOMETIMES OUR PSYCHIC ABILITIES BRING US INFORmation about what is going to happen in the future. This phenomenon is called precognition, and it occurs in both the dreaming and waking states of consciousness.

In 1898 Morgan Robertson wrote a story called "The Wreck of the *Titan.*" In it a huge ocean liner, the *Titan,* was steaming through the icy mid-Atlantic in April. The ship was described as being 800 feet (244 m) long, having a speed of 25 knots, and having a passenger capacity of well over 3,000. Yet it had only 24 lifeboats, far too few for a ship of its size. Suddenly the ship rammed an iceberg and sank, leaving 3,000 people struggling and screaming in the icy waters.

Perhaps the most interesting aspect of this story concerns the manner in which it was written. Robertson claimed that ideas for stories would come to him as visions when he was in a trance state. He believed that these visions came to him from an "astral writing partner," a kind of psychic spirit.

At 2:20 A.M. on the morning of April 15, 1912, the world's largest "unsinkable" ocean liner collided at full speed with an iceberg that ripped a huge gash in its bow and sank it. Hundreds of passengers struggled into the too few life boats, and 1,500 others were lost with the ship. The name of the ship was the *Titanic.*

Was this mere coincidence? A good guess? Or precognition? Some researchers feel that the similarities between Robertson's story and the details of the disaster might have arisen from good guesswork. Robertson had studied shipbuilding. He might have guessed the direction in which future design was headed (his description of the physical features of the ship were very close to those of the *Titanic*); he might have predicted that a tragedy would befall the latest of man's engineering marvels; and he might have even guessed the nature of the tragedy. We will never know for sure.

But, Robertson's story was not the only psychic event that surrounded the sinking of the *Titanic.*

Among the many spectators who watched the *Titanic* set out on its maiden voyage from Southampton to New York were a Mr. and Mrs. Jack Marshall. With the *Titanic* still in view, Mrs. Marshall grabbed her husband's arm and shouted, "That ship is going to sink before she reaches America." Her husband tried to calm her. Friends who were with them tried to explain to her that the *Titanic* had been built by a completely new method that made it unsinkable.

Her daughter, Joan Grant, was there when the incident occurred, and she recorded her mother's response in her book *Far Memory:*

"Don't just stand there staring at me! Do something! You fools, I can see hundreds of people struggling in the icy water! Are you all so blind that you are going to let them drown?"

12

Indeed, the builders of the *Titanic had* announced that the ship was unsinkable. It had a double bottom and fifteen watertight bulkheads, which could be closed to seal off the rest of the ship. Unfortunately, these were not enough to prevent the catastrophe. When the ship rammed the iceberg, water rushed into the forward compartments and tipped the bow; two and a half hours later the *Titanic* slid under the waves.

On the same day that Mrs. Marshall had her vision, a Mr. V. N. Turvey also predicted that a "great liner will be lost." Turvey was a sensitive—a person who is highly endowed with psychic abilities. On April 13 he wrote a letter to a friend telling her of his prediction. He claimed the ship would sink in two days.

Ten days before the *Titanic* sailed, J. Connon Middleton had a dream. He saw a ship "floating on the sea, keel upward and her passengers and crew swimming around her." Later he had a second vision of disaster. This time he himself was "floating in the air just above the wreck."

According to Andrew Mackenzie, in *Riddle of the Future,* Mr. Middleton disregarded these nocturnal warnings. However, he subsequently received a cable from the United States instructing him, for business reasons, to delay his sailing for several days. Mrs. Middleton later testified that her husband had said "how foolish it would seem if he postponed his business on account of a dream." As Mackenzie states, "If the cable from New York had not arrived he would presumably have sailed in the *Titanic* and possibly perished."

13

W. T. Stead, distinguished journalist, editor, and spiritualist, was not so lucky. Stead was told by Count Harmon, a sensitive with whom he conferred while on vacation, that danger to his life would come from water, nothing else. In June 1911 the sensitive wrote Stead advising him that "travel would be dangerous to him in the month of April, 1912."

In *Riddle of the Future* Andrew Mackenzie goes on to explain that Stead also consulted with another sensitive, Mr. W. de Kerlor. De Kerlor received an impression of a half-completed black ship. The sensitive interpreted this vision to mean that when the ship was completed, Stead would go on a voyage. Later de Kerlor dreamed about an oceanic catastrophe. He found himself surrounded by "masses of bodies struggling in the water," he could hear their cries for help. He felt that his dream concerned Mr. Stead and told him about it. De Kerlor was worried, first by a black ship, and now by a seaborne disaster.

Mr. Stead is reported to have said, "Oh, yes; well, well, you are a very gloomy prophet." He sailed with the *Titanic*—and he was lost with it.

When so many different people have similar precognitive experiences over a long period of time, it leads one to believe that these glimpses into the future are more than mere coincidence. In fact, it leads one to believe that people really can "see" into the future.

We have seen examples of telepathy, clairvoyance, and precognition at work in daily life and in the laboratory. As a group, these three psychic processes provide us with a natural resource that almost begs to be put to work. How can we best use these psychic

14

resources? For the criminologist the answer is clear; telepathy, clairvoyance, and precognition can be used as uniquely effective investigatory tools in the fight against crime.

The telepathic "reading" of suspects' minds allows police to tune in to the suspects' innermost thoughts and to determine the truth or falsity of alibis, as well as providing clues to direct the search for hard evidence—evidence acceptable in a court of law. (The psychic's telepathic knowledge of suspects' guilt is not enough to convict.)

Clairvoyant impressions triggered by visiting the scene of a crime or by handling a crime related photograph or object can provide information about the identity of the criminal, his *modus operandi* (MO), his motives, and his whereabouts. Sometimes the psychic, relying on clairvoyant impressions, can actually relive the crime, observing the action *as it took place*.

Precognitive impressions can be used to warn police of *future* criminal acts and crimes still in the planning stages, thereby allowing the police to take the necessary preventive steps.

The extrasensory abilities of the psychic detective are invaluable crimefighting tools. They can provide police with information that, in many cases, is impossible to obtain in any other way.

Do psychic detectives really have these abilities? Does anyone? Are telepathy, clairvoyance, and precognition *real*? Let's see what the scientists have to say.

SCIENCE AND PSYCHICS

IN THE NOT TOO DISTANT PAST, WHENEVER THE WORD "psychic" was mentioned, scientists and laymen alike would conjure up the picture of a séance with quack mediums, darkened rooms, floating tables, voices of spirits, automatic writing, crystal balls, Ouija boards, and so on.

To rational men and women these melodramatic events were easy to dismiss. Wasn't it obvious that these so-called psychic events were really the tricks of magicians and showmen? Certainly a respectable scientist would never even begin to consider the likes of such nonsense. There was much more serious work to be done; these matters were best left to the fools who either believed in or enjoyed them.

Fortunately, not all scientists felt this way.

Perhaps out of curiosity or perhaps on the word of a good friend whose truthfulness was beyond question, the scientists began to explore the world of the medium. To their surprise, they discovered that not all were quacks: some mediums, in addition to being honest and sincere, seemed to have real psychic ability.

In the late 1800s English scientists got together to experiment with the then new concept of telepathy. They tried to "send" drawings to especially gifted subjects. In the results of a single telepathy session they found that certain subjects could indeed "receive" the drawings.

Experiments like these were carried out by members of the British Society for Psychical Research, which was founded in 1882. Many of these men were highly respected and world-renowned scientists, philosophers, and critical thinkers. Their studies were carried out in serious and rigorous fashion, and their collective work established a very strong case for the existence of psychic phenomena.

In our own country, early researchers, led by J. B. Rhine at Duke University, worked hard to establish incontrovertible proof of the reality of these phenomena. They wanted parapsychology to be accepted as a legitimate aspect of scientific knowledge, and they wanted psychic events accepted as legitimate phenomena of the natural world.

These researchers bent over backward to erase the emotionalism associated with the séance and the sense of drama surrounding the occult. They wanted to provide hard scientific data—unbiased, irrefutable evidence. They wanted to build a scientifically acceptable case, one that would be so strong that other scientists would *have* to accept the evidence for psychic phenomena.

Rhine and his coworkers explored telepathy, clairvoyance, and precognition using card-guessing experiments. Special ESP cards, called Zener Cards, were used. Each deck had twenty-five cards divided into five suits: stars, crosses, squares, circles, and wavy lines. There were five of each.

In the experiments the subject had to try to guess which card another subject was thinking about, or which card had been selected by random shuffling, or which card would be selected by a future shuffle. Rhine and his colleagues recorded the subjects' results very carefully, documenting the numbers of hits and misses during each run.

The Zener Cards were used because they made it easier to evaluate the success of the subjects' "guesses." By chance alone anyone should be able to correctly guess five of the twenty-five cards. The problem was to determine exactly how many correct guesses it would take to demonstrate that something other than chance was at work. Six? Eight? Eighteen?

Fortunately for Rhine by the late 1920s the field of statistics had developed a way of answering this question precisely. As Louisa E. Rhine explains in *Psi: What Is It?*, parapsychologists could, by then, use a statistical formula to calculate exactly when their results were "better than chance" and when they were good enough to be calculated as "significant."

This was a completely new development in

19

paraspychological research. Instead of guesswork, experimenters could, from then on, analyze and explain their results in precise mathematical terms. This brought their work to a new level: it became much more acceptable scientifically. The parapsychologist could finally use the same laws of statistics and probability that the mathematician and physicist relied on—and the results were overwhelming.

Time and again Rhine's carefully documented and analyzed experiments showed that something other than chance was at work in the parapsychology laboratory. Subjects were found that could score a number of hits that were millions, and sometimes billions, of times greater than chance alone allowed for.

To account for these successful hits Rhine concluded that his subjects must have received information to help them with their guesses. Since the experiments were designed to prevent information from traveling through the five regular senses, Rhine concluded that *extra*sensory perception must have been at work.

It is important to understand that the manner in which Rhine and his coworkers arrived at their conclusions utilized the same methods that their colleagues, working in less controversial sciences, used. They built theories, ran experiments, collected results, and then analyzed these results mathematically. It was precisely these mathematically-based conclusions that convinced so many skeptical scientists that ESP was real.

But the acceptance of the evidence did not take place overnight. At first many scientists could not, or would not, accept it. Some scientists wouldn't even bother to look at the evidence in the first place. They were like the clergymen who refused to look through Galileo's telescope at the craters on the moon because they *knew* that the moon and all the other heavenly bodies were perfect—and perfect bodies didn't have craters, especially if they were made of crystal.

Among those scientists who did take the trouble to examine the evidence, many were not ready to examine it objectively. They could not believe that extrasensory perception was a possibility: it was not *supposed* to exist, so it simply *could not* exist. These scientists claimed that there was either something wrong with the "facts" about ESP or the ways in which they were obtained. For them the so-called facts of psychic research were due to coincidence, faulty memory, unrecognized "normal" causes, faulty experiments, imagination, hallucination, fraud, trickery, lies, conspiracy—anything, but not ESP.

Others eventually realized that the evidence in favor of ESP was too strong to dismiss. But they *still* couldn't bring themselves to accept it. Many probably felt like the mathematician Warren Weaver. As Arthur Koestler reports in *Roots of Coincidence,* Weaver once said, "I find this [ESP] a subject that is so intellectually uncomfortable as to be almost painful. I end by concluding that I cannot explain away Professor Rhine's evidence, and that I also cannot accept his interpretation."

Rhine and his colleagues continued with their work; they continued to strengthen their already solid body of evidence until the case for the existence

21

of psychic phenomena grew so strong that it could no longer be ignored. In 1969 the American Society for the Advancement of Science finally recognized the Parapsychology Association, thereby granting its seal of approval.

Why did it take so long? Why were psychic phenomena, and the science that studied them, so difficult for the scientific community to accept? Any new idea takes time to be accepted, but the nature of ESP has made it doubly hard for scientists to swallow it.

To begin with, psychic events are seemingly rare, unpredictable, and capricious: they are not under voluntary control. In most cases they cannot be summoned at will. Instead they are unconsciously controlled. They just happen. We can of course try to discover which situations favor their occurrence, but we cannot make them happen, or guarantee that they will happen.

This state of affairs is most disturbing to the scientist. Scientists like to work with subjects that are both repeatable and predictable, and this is precisely what psychic phenomena are *not*. Even with the best of subjects—people who successfully demonstrate psychic abilities time and again—there is no way to ensure that on the morning of a particular experiment the subjects will be able to generate their abilities.

In fact, the attempt to consciously produce psychic phenomena in the laboratory may be the very thing that prevents them from occurring. At the same time the atmosphere of the lab, the state of mind of the experimenters, and the nature of the test material all have a great effect on the ability of the subject to "work." A skeptical, "show-me" attitude on the part of the researchers, coupled with a feeling of being put to the test, may create a self-defeating emotional mood and make it that much more difficult to generate psychic effects, as will an uninteresting experiment.

Although these factors made it difficult to study ESP in the laboratory, there were even greater hurdles to be overcome before ESP could be recognized. The problem was that psychic phenomena appeared to contradict the basic world view held by most scientists and laymen alike—a world view that resulted from a union of common sense and outdated scientific beliefs.

In the seventeenth century Sir Isaac Newton invented a description of the universe that ruled scientific thought for over two hundred years. It was the basis for what is now called classical physics. His ideas were based upon a philosophy that originated in ancient Greece and had been reinforced by the French philosopher René Descartes. The basic idea of this philosophy was that everything in the universe could be divided into two separate categories, mind and matter.

Using this philosophy scientists felt justified in viewing matter (the "stuff" of the world) as essentially lifeless, completely separated from themselves, and totally unaffected by their thoughts and feelings. Built of small solid particles, matter was thought to be organized into a machinelike universe: each event had a definite cause and gave rise to a

23

definite effect. This universe had been set in motion by divine power and was thereafter ruled by unchangeable laws.

This Newtonian world was one in which space was at rest and unchangeable, in which time always flowed like a river from past to present to future, in its own special dimension, unconnected to the material world.

This model of the universe held out the hope of absolute knowledge for man. He had only to figure out the laws of the "machine" once and for all, and he would know everything there was to know forever. The work of science was envisioned as being that of putting together a giant jigsaw puzzle; you worked and worked and, eventually, you got to see *the* picture.

For over two centuries it seemed as though man might indeed unravel this universal puzzle. Newton and his successors used his theories to explain the basic features of our solar system, the motion of the planets, the motion of fluids, the vibration of elastic bodies, heat, and so on.

In addition to being practically and theoretically successful, Newton's mechanical model of the universe was easy to picture. It also fit our commonsense notion of things.

We human beings are accustomed to a medium-sized existence on our planet Earth. We are used to dealing with things that are not too large and not too small and with things that do not move very quickly, as motion in the universe goes. Common sense tells us that the world is filled with "things":

24

people, plants, animals, and a host of lifeless objects, such as ordinary pebbles and rocks. We speak about a rock as being a solid "thing," one that has color, shape, form, and perhaps taste. A rock seems to sit in front of us very quietly. We can describe its location in space and time very accurately. The way it appears to us seems to be totally independent from, and unaffected by, our presence.

Newtonian physics and common sense made a powerful union. It was against *their* joint world view that psychic phenomena appeared to be misfits of the highest order—unscientific, annoying, ridiculous, and finally, absolutely impossible.

But this world view died over a hundred years ago, leaving only its ghost to prejudice current scientific inquiry. It was discarded when the physicist began to explore the vastness of the universe and the infinitesimal dimensions of the atom and the nucleus. Once he left the familiar boundaries of the everyday world, the scientist was forced to leave common sense and Newton behind.

For today's physicist a rock appears to be quite a different creature than that pictured by Newton. For physicists today the "rockness" of the rock disappears before their eyes. When they rip it apart, penetrate its atoms and nuclei and then the pieces that make up the nuclei, they find that "things" lose their "thingness."

They discover that the rock is mostly empty space; that it is colorless, odorless, soundless, and tasteless. The familiar protons, electrons, and neutrons give way to a host of smaller particles, which themselves seem to turn into energy before our eyes and become impossible to pinpoint in terms of space and time. In fact, a physicist doesn't even speak of rock-matter as existing anymore. Instead they say it "tends" to exist. And they never say that atomic events within the rock will happen with *certainty;* they only tell us their *probability* of occurring.

In addition it is no longer possible to speak about the scientist as a detached and objective observer. In order to "see" into the atomic world the scientist must become involved with it, so much so that today's physicist actually influences the properties of whatever it is he is investigating.

As explained by physicist John Wheeler, the quantum theory destroys the notion of the world as "sitting out there" separated from the scientist by a "twenty-centimeter (7.87-inch) slab of plate glass." In order to observe an electron the scientist must break through the glass, reach in, and set up measuring devices. But these devices, in order to locate and then clock the electron's movements, will have to change the state of the electron itself. As quoted by Fritjof Capra in the *Tao of Physics,* Wheeler comments that

> the universe will never afterwards be the same. To describe what has happened, one has to cross out that old word "observer" and put in its place the new word "participator." In some strange sense the universe is a participatory universe.

In the atomic realm it becomes impossible to believe that separated pieces, distinct "building blocks,"

26

are the ultimate reality of the universe. The concept of separate particles dissolves before our very eyes— our mind's eyes, more precisely. In the atomic world there are no particles. Instead, the particle and its background quantum field seem to blend into one whole.

The advances in the quantum theory have forced us to envision the universe as a complex web of unbroken wholeness; not as a collection of separate physical objects, but as the web of relations between the parts of a whole. The idea of the isolated particle is just an intellectual abstraction. We can only observe the "particle" and its properties when it *interacts* with another part of the universe. By itself, it does not exist. Instead of *things* we find *connections*.

Then, too, it is impossible to "see" anything in this world without bringing the conscious mind of the scientist into account. The particular theories (and equipment) that the scientist uses drastically affect both what he can see and what he will see.

In the high-speed nuclear world, time itself loses its familiar qualities. Seen through Einstein's theory of relativity, it becomes welded to the three dimensions of space to produce a four-dimensional universe, and it is very much affected by worldly events such as motion and gravity.

Time appears to slow down for the rapidly moving nuclear particles. In addition some scientists have proposed that it loses its one-way character. Richard Phillipps Feynman won a Nobel prize for his theories that included antiparticles moving *backward* in time.

As you can see, the physicist has created a com-

27

pletely new picture of reality: one that has violated all the old laws. It is one that is not easily envisioned or understood. It is one that the senses cannot penetrate. It is one that relies instead on intricate theory and complex mathematical symbols in order to see, explain, and guide further exploration of a universe that, as Sir James Jeans has said, "begins to look more like a great thought than a great machine."

Seen against this "anything goes" attitude of the new physics, the phenomena of the psychic world —telepathy, clairvoyance, and precognition—seem much less bizarre and improbable. The new physics has created a climate of possibility, an openness to radically new ideas, which has made it easier to accept the reality of ESP.

Ironically, the picture of reality painted by the most recent advances in modern physics is strikingly similar to the age-old wisdom of the East, as embodied in the philosophical thoughts of Hinduism, Buddhism, Taoism, and Zen.

In *The Tao of Physics* Fritjof Capra illustrates this point with a quote from noted physicist Niels Bohr.

> For a parallel to the lesson of atomic theory . . . [we must turn] to those kinds of . . . [philosophical] problems with which . . . thinkers like the Buddha and Lao Tzu have been confronted, when trying to harmonize our position as spectators and actors in the great drama of existence.

As Capra explains, the most important characteristic of the Eastern world view is an awareness of the basic unity of all things and events. "All things are seen as interdependent and inseparable parts of this cosmic whole; as different manifestations of the same ultimate reality." In Hinduism this ultimate reality is called *Brahman*, in Buddhism it is *Dharmakaya*, in Taoism it is *Tao*.

The goal of Eastern religion is to quiet the mind through meditation, to pierce through the illusions of everyday life, and to experience the ultimate reality directly. The Eastern mystic does not rely on his intellect of senses to attain "Absolute" knowledge of this reality. Instead he experiences reality in what we might call a "nonordinary state of consciousness"— a meditative or mystical state.

In any event this ultimate reality is experienced as being the driving force behind the ever changing universe that we perceive in daily life, "forever in motion, alive, organic, spiritual and material at the same time." Ultimate reality manifests itself in terms of opposites and paradoxes: hot and cold, good and evil, light and dark, male and female, living and nonliving, past and future, matter and mind. But these opposites only *appear* to be such because we are ignorant. For the mystic who has attained enlightenment these opposites are experienced as being connected, as being merely different manifestations of the same basic reality, always changing, and yet always the same.

Capra goes on to explain that Eastern thought regards the intellectual concepts we use to describe nature—space, time, cause and effect, wave, particle—as being fundamentally limited. These categories

29

and concepts are *not* parts of reality, as we often like to believe, but rather creations of our minds. Capra compares these concepts to maps: concepts are like manmade maps (*symbols*) of reality, not the territory (*reality*) itself. This is a view that modern physics has come to share.

Finally, as Lawrence LeShan points out in *The Medium, the Mystic, and the Physicist,* the picture of reality created by Eastern mystics and physicists corresponds to the descriptions of reality provided by sensitives when they are undergoing *psychic* experiences. This is especially true in terms of the oneness and interconnectedness of the universe, both of which are perceived without reliance upon sense, common sense, or an intellectual understanding of the universe we live in.

Parapsychology is still very young as sciences go. At present it is unable to explain the precise nature of telepathy, clairvoyance, or precognition. Parapsychologists do not know *how* these phenomena work. There is comparably little in the way of theory, and what theory there is has not been universally accepted as an adequate explanation of the workings of the psychic processes. Parapsychologists still can't tell us how the psychic detective reads minds, receives clairvoyant visions, or peeks into the future.

However, the acceptance of ESP by the scientific establishment, and the consequent intensification of research efforts being undertaken, may well lead to the solution of the mysteries of psychic phenomena, with profound long term effects on our own society.

As H. H. Price, an Oxford University professor of philosophy, has stated:

> . . . Psychical research is one of the most important branches of investigation which the human mind has undertaken. . . . it seems likely to throw entirely new light upon the nature of human personality and its position in the universe. . . . [in time] it may transform the whole intellectual outlook upon which our present civilization is based.

Once the mysteries are unraveled, we can expect to develop more sophisticated and efficient ways of making ESP work for us, especially in the fight against crime.

ESP, then, is, a real, scientifically acceptable phenomenon. Where has it been hiding? Have people been using ESP? What was ESP up to two thousand years ago? Are there cultures that rely on ESP today?

OTHER TIMES —— OTHER WORLDS

WHEN SHOULD WE PLANT? SHOULD WE GO TO WAR? Is it time for the harvest? What should we do? What does it mean? These were some of the questions asked of the seer, the oracle, the diviner, the witch doctor, and the shaman—all of whom were recognized for their ability to see into that other reality and contact the spirits of gods, animals, and ancestors. All were thought to be endowed with the gifts of prophecy or precognition—the ability to foretell the future—and were therefore relied upon to guide the actions of the community. In many cases, the community's very survival depended upon the accuracy of these prophets' advice.

In biblical times dreams were often thought of as being precognitive messages from the future—mes-

33

sages that could only be understood by a gifted dream interpreter.

One night the pharaoh of Egypt had a dream in which seven fat, fleshy kine (cattle) were eaten by seven lean kine. In a second dream he saw seven full ears of corn come up on a single stalk. They were followed by seven thin and wasted ears. The thin ears swallowed up the full ones. The pharaoh was greatly perplexed by his dreams. He summoned all the wise men and magicians in his kingdom, but none could interpret his troubling dreams.

Finally he was told that a man being held in his prison was a gifted interpreter. He summoned the man at once and described his dreams in detail. The man, Joseph, understood the meaning of the dreams immediately. It was a warning to the people of Egypt. The fleshy kine and full ears of corn represented seven bountiful years, years of plentiful harvests. The lean kine and the wasted ears of corn represented a famine that would follow.

Joseph interpreted the dreams for the pharaoh and then instructed him to send his emissaries throughout the land to collect and store food during the years of plenty. The pharaoh followed Joseph's advice. When the years of poor harvest followed, his people were saved from the famine.

In ancient Egypt it was also common practice to write letters to the dead. Some of these letters date back to the year 2400 B.C. The Egyptians strongly believed in the existence of the spirit world. They thought that the spirits of the dead knew about events in our earthly world. They also thought that they could

34

communicate with these spirits. In addition to letters the Egyptians had mediums, who, in much the same manner as modern spiritualists, believed they could contact these spirits during séances.

Oracles played an important role in the lives of ancient Greeks. The word "oracle" referred to the practice of obtaining messages from the gods: the oracle would ask questions of the gods and receive the divine replies.

One of the most famous oracles was at Delphi, which was dedicated to the god Apollo. At Delphi the person who contacted the gods was a woman known as Pythia.

Before the gods could be questioned at Delphi precise rituals had to be performed, including a carefully prescribed animal sacrifice. After the sacrifice Pythia would drink from a sacred spring, and then she would return to the basement of the temple. There she would rise to the sacred tripod and chew the leaves of the Laurel tree.

Eventually Pythia would enter a trance state. Words would flow from her uncontrollably. These utterings would be interpreted and recorded by priests. Often the priests' interpretations were couched in highly ambiguous language.

These inspired prophets were often considered somewhat mad: it was a madness which can probably be explained by their apparent loss of control when possessed by the power of the gods. For Socrates this madness was a "special gift of heaven, and the source of the chiefest blessing among men. . . ."

The ancient prophets didn't always make correct

interpretations or predictions. If they failed, they risked losing their positions of importance, even worse, they risked banishment from the community.

Fortunately the prophets weren't always required to answer questions of grave import that were directly concerned with the affairs of state. Much of their time was taken up with questions about everyday affairs. Archeologists have uncovered tablets with questions like: Have I lost my blankets and pillows myself, or has someone stolen them? Am I the father of my wife's child?

The Greek tragedian Euripides tells the story of the war against Troy to recapture Helen. Helen was the wife of King Menelaus. The Greek army was gathered at Aulis and ready to sail, but the winds would not blow. The men were restless. Then the priest Calchus came to King Agamemnon with the words of the oracle: Agamemnon must sacrifice his own firstborn child. Then, and only then, would the winds blow. Only then would the Greek army be victorious in war. Agamemnon's daughter was sacrificed to the gods and the ships set sail, and the Greek army conquered Troy.

In *ESP and the Clairvoyants* R. Van Over explains that divination has an even older history in the East. In China especially it has always been a respected art. Pieces of stone and bone from the eleventh century B.C. have been found that tell of the different methods used to foretell the future. The entrails of birds and their patterns of flight were carefully studied, as were smoke patterns. All were thought to carry information about the future.

The use of mediums was also common. It was

believed that spirits could take over the body of the human medium and speak through him or her. The spirits would both give advice and cure illness.

Today psychic abilities continue to play important roles in many so-called primitive societies— the aborigines of Australia, the Navajo of the American Southwest, the Azandi of Africa, the Tungus of the Arctic lands, the Akawaio of British Guiana, the Semai Senoi of Malaya, and so on.

Among these peoples it is commonly believed that communication with the spirit world is best achieved while in a state of trance—a state in which normal consciousness is altered and the person appears to enter a new dimension of space and time. A variety of methods was developed to achieve this state: isolation, starvation, dance, chant, and the rhythm of the drum were all used.

In the Middle East the whirling dervishes dance faster and faster, until one of their number falls to the floor and experiences visions. African and Australian tribesmen rely on the rhythms of drum and chant to induce the trance. Among Central American Indians plants are used to prepare special brews that help induce the trance. The bark of certain trees, jungle vines, and wild tobacco are all used to make the drug-filled potions.

In *The Probability of the Impossible* Dr. Thelma Moss relates the following story about Dr. William McGovern who took *caapi*, a jungle vine concoction, with the natives of an Amazon village.

Certain of the Indians fell into a particularly deep state of trance, in which they appeared to possess

37

telepathic powers. . . . On this particular evening, the local medicine man told me that the chief of a certain tribe in the far away Pira Pirana had suddenly died. I entered this statement in my diary and many weeks later, when we came to the tribe in question, I found that the witch doctor's statement had been true in every detail. Possibly these cases were mere coincidence.

A second account is reported by R. L. Van de Castle in his article, "The Cuna Indians of Panama." In it Father Trilles relates the story of his encounter with Negema Nzago, chief and "celebrated fetish man" (witch doctor) of the Yabakou tribe.

One day the shaman told Father Trilles that he was going to a meeting of all the magicians at a far-off, abandoned village. Father Trilles knew that the village was a four-day march away, yet the shaman said he would be there the next evening. "You do not believe me: well . . . come to my hut. I shall leave from there."

When the missionary arrived at Nzago's hut he asked the shaman to deliver a message to a friend who lived in a distant village. "As you pass before his door . . . tell him that I must see him, that he should come at once and bring me the cartridges of the shotgun which I gave him to keep." The shaman said he would deliver the message.

Then the shaman began to prepare himself for the trip. He rubbed himself all over with a red liquid that smelled of garlic. He began chanting. Suddenly Father Trilles saw a large snake slip from the roof of the hut and curl around the shaman's body. Soon the shaman fell asleep.

Father Trilles noticed that the shaman's body was perfectly rigid. He stuck a pin into his flesh but the shaman didn't even flinch. (The snake had departed by this time.) Father Trilles observed a white, foamy substance on the shaman's lips.

Father Trilles passed the entire night in the shaman's hut. He did not leave it for an instant. The following morning the magician woke up and spoke to Father Trilles. "I have given your message," he said, and then went on to describe the meeting of magicians in which he had participated.

Several days later a man arrived with a message for Father Trilles. "Here are the cartridges which you sent for by the magician."

"What?" Father Trilles said, "Did you see him?"

"No," the man replied, "but I heard him during the night, and he called me from outside my hut and told me that you wanted these at once."

The aborigines of Australia are primitive tribesmen who live in the wilderness under Stone Age conditions. Their normal senses are reported to be unusually highly developed. According to R. Van Over they can see small objects at great distances, hear sounds that civilized man cannot pick up, and can even tell the difference between a man and a small animal by the sense of smell.

In addition to their highly developed normal senses, the aborigines are reported to be unusually sensitive to psychic phenomena.

Psychologist Lyndon Rose in conjunction with Sydney University, conducted psychic tests of the aborigines of northern New South Wales. In one test Rose put a cigarette into a sealed box. Ten miles away three aborigines were asked to describe the contents of the box. One said cigarette, the other two said tobacco and paper. In another test a cigarette holder was added to the box. Nine out of ten of the people tested described the shape, length, and color of the holder, an object they had never seen before.

Here in our own country, in 1960 Carlos Castaneda, a young graduate student in anthropology, was collecting information about certain plants that were used by Indians in their medicines and mystical potions. He was introduced to Don Juan, a Yaqui Indian who was supposed to be a *brujo*, or sorcerer, and who was very knowledgeable about plants.

After meeting with and talking to him during the following year, the young man was asked to become the *brujo's* apprentice. He was to learn the Indian traditions of sorcery and become a "Man of Knowledge."

Could a man raised in a modern western culture enter the nonordinary reality of the sorcerer? How would the world appear to him? How would he explain his experiences?

Castaneda's apprenticeship triggered a clash of cultures and philosophies that proved painful in many ways. His encounters with the sorcerer's reality were intellectually and emotionally jarring. This "other reality" was difficult to accept, and yet, impossible to dismiss.

Toward the end of his first period of apprenticeship Castaneda had an experience in which he felt he was flying. (It is what scientists would probably call an out-of-body experience, in which the consciousness appears to detach itself from the physical body and travel free.)

After inhaling one of Don Juan's special herbal mixtures, Castaneda took off.

> ... I soared ... I saw the dark sky above me, and the clouds going by me. I jerked my body so I could look down. I saw the dark mass of the mountains. My speed was extraordinary. ... I enjoyed such freedom and swiftness as I had never known before.

Eventually he landed. He realized that he was about a half mile (.8 km) from Don Juan's house. It was early morning. He was completely naked. Someone was coming up the road. He hid behind some bushes until he recognized Don Juan carrying his clothes. He had one question to ask his teacher: "Did I really fly, Don Juan? ... I mean, did my body fly? Did I take off like a bird?"

Casteneda wanted to know if his experience was *real* or just a hallucination or a strange lifelike dream. Don Juan replied:

> The trouble with you is that you understand things in only one way. . . .
> ... The world we perceive, though, is an illusion. It was created by a description that was told to us since the moment we were born. . . .
> ... The world is such-and-such ... only because we tell ourselves that that is the way it is. If we stop telling ourselves that the world is so-and-so, the world will stop being so-and-so.

For Don Juan there are several realities. De-

41

pending upon which one you enter, the world will assume any of its several disguises, each having its own rules and boundaries concerning what is possible and impossible.

> Gregorio washed his hands and arms, rolled up his sleeves to the elbows, and went to the top of a hill. He faced north, the direction in which the handbag had been lost, and sprinkled corn pollen on his right hand. The hand soon started to tremble. Then he rubbed the palm of his left hand with the palm of his right; the left hand started to tremble instead . . . with his eyes shut, Gregorio began to make motions with both hands symbolizing the missing bag. He said it had been left at a local trading post.

The above incident took place in 1937. The handbag belonged to the wife of Clyde Kluckhorn, a famous anthropologist. The man, Gregorio, was a Navajo Indian hand trembler who practiced a form of divination that continues to be used in the present day.

As Richard Reichbart points out in his article, "The Navajo Hand Trembler," the hand trembler performs a wide variety of functions for his tribesmen. He is the finder of lost and stolen objects as well as criminals. He is also a "psychic detective" in cases of bewitchment, locating the object of witchcraft that is usually buried beneath the hogan (living quarters) of the victim. In addition he is a diagnostician in the Navajo medical system, where his job is to discover which taboo was broken or to determine the meaning of a dream that is thought to have been the cause of illness.

In the past the hand trembler was relied on to find water when the tribe was in a strange land. He also had to predict the outcome of a particular war raid or hunt.

Once Dr. Robert Bergman, chief psychiatrist of the Indian Health Service, was demonstrating hypnosis to a group of medicine men. He hypnotized a woman, caused her to hallucinate, and she acted as if she were a very young girl.

The medicine men recognized the similarity between the hypnotic state and the trance of the hand trembler. They asked Dr. Bergman to let the woman perform a medical diagnosis the way a hand trembler would do in *his* trance state. Dr. Bergman didn't like the idea of a medical diagnosis but agreed instead to let the woman do a weather prediction. The woman told the group about the rainfall for the next six months. Dr. Bergman commented that "she was precisely correct."

On witnessing this demonstration one medicine man had this to say:

> I'm 82 years old, and I've seen white people all my life, but this is the first time that one has ever surprised me. I'm not surprised to see something like this happen because we do things like this, but I am surprised that a white man should know anything so worthwhile.

ACCIDENTAL MEETINGS

TRADITIONALLY WE HAVE RELIED ON SCIENCE AND technology to help us explore and develop the environment around us. We have directed our attention and our resources toward the conquest of the land, the taming of the seas, and the exploration of outer space.

But while conquering the world around us, we have neglected the world within. As a result we actually know very little about the capacities and potentials of inner space: the realm of subconscious and psychic functioning.

In the past this ignorance of inner space allowed many of us to regard psychic abilities as childish superstition and psychics as kooks, weirdos, and phonies. Many but not all of us felt this way. There have always been *some* people who believed that ESP was real. Sometimes this suspicion was confirmed when a person experienced a psychic episode of his or her own. At other times it was confirmed by encountering firsthand evidence of the psychic abilities of another.

Ironically, over the years there have been many such accidental encounters between the police and individuals who claimed to have experienced crime-related psychic visions. A stranger might walk in off the street and offer information about a crime to come; a crime he had *already* witnessed. At other times the identity of a murderer might be provided by a psychic entertainer, for example, a mind reader or a fortune teller. At still other times it might come from so-called genuine psychics—men and women who had established impeccable reputations as practitioners of the psychic sciences.

One day in the autumn of 1888 Robert James Lees was at work in his study, when, quite suddenly, he experienced a psychic vision. In *Crime and the Psychic World* Fred Archer reports that Lees saw a man and woman strolling down a deserted street. The woman appeared drunk, the man sober. After walking a short distance they turned into a narrow court, where they sought refuge in a dark corner.

The man, dressed in a dark tweed suit and carrying a light overcoat, stepped closer to the woman. He glanced around quickly to make sure they were alone, then slapped his hand over the woman's mouth.

The woman struggled, but he was too strong for

46

her. Before she could utter a single muffled cry the man pulled out his knife and killed her.

Still covering her mouth with his hand, he lowered the body to the ground.

When he had completed his work he calmly wiped the blade on her dress, put it away, slipped on his overcoat, and slowly walked away.

R. J. Lees was "a man of private means, a scholar, and a philanthropist." He was a "gentle mystic," a man more interested in explaining the fine points of the Bible than in bringing criminals to justice. His religious writings were well known by bishops and cardinals. He was a friend of both Gladstone and Disraeli, who were British prime ministers under Queen Victoria. Above all else, his word was respected unquestioningly by those who knew him.

Robert James Lees was sure that his vision of murder had not yet taken place. He proceeded to do what any other good citizen would have done: he went straight to Scotland Yard. Unfortunately the officer at the desk regarded him as just another crank. To humor him the officer took down his description of the crime and sent him home.

The next night the murder was committed. Lees went to the scene of the crime and nearly had a nervous collapse. It was the same court he had seen in his vision. It upset him so much that he couldn't sleep at night. His physician suggested that he go abroad for a rest, which he did.

In a short while he recovered his health and returned to London. One afternoon he and his wife were

47

on their way home when a man wearing a dark tweed suit and light overcoat boarded the bus. Startled, Lees turned to his wife and said: "That man is Jack the Ripper."

When the man got off the bus Lees followed him. After a few minutes Lees saw a policeman. He ran up to him and explained that the man up ahead was the Ripper and had to be arrested. The policeman looked at Lees as if he were a lunatic, and the man in the tweed suit hopped a cab and disappeared.

That very evening Lees had a second vision: he saw another woman murdered. This time he could see the victim's face clearly. One ear had been cut off, the other hung by a thread.

Again the gentle mystic traveled to Scotland Yard. This time he demanded a meeting with a chief inspector. Skeptical at first, the inspector changed his attitude when Lees described the victim's ears. Earlier in the day the police had been forwarded a letter in which a person claiming to be Jack the Ripper boasted he would "clip the lady's ears off" and present them to the police.

The inspector increased police protection, but it didn't help. The Ripper managed to strike again and vanish into the night with two more victims.

Apparently, he must have seen someone coming, and, afraid of being discovered, he left his first victim before he completed his handiwork: he had only begun to sever the woman's ears.

Not too long after Lees had a third vision. He was at dinner with a friend when he suddenly shouted

48

that Jack the Ripper had just committed another murder.

When he went to the Yard this time he was asked if there were some way he could help to track down the killer. Lees agreed to try.

He was taken to the scene of the latest crime. Once there he tried to pick up the "scent." Eventually he led the police through the streets of London toward the well-to-do West End section. Finally he stopped in front of an imposing mansion. He turned to the inspector and told him he would find the Ripper inside.

The inspector couldn't believe it. The home belonged to a well-known and respected doctor.

Uncertain about how to proceed, the inspector asked Lees to describe the inside of the mansion. The inspector decided he would enter it, and if it matched Lees's description, he would proceed with the investigation.

Lees immediately provided the details: a porter's chair of black oak to the right, a stained glass window at one end, and a large dog, a mastiff, sleeping at the foot of the stairs.

The inspector knocked on the door, was let in, and found the scene exactly as Lees had described, except for the dog. There was none. He surprised the maid by asking about its whereabouts. She replied that it had just been sleeping at the foot of the stairs before she had let it out for a run.

The inspector then asked to speak to the doctor's wife. The woman was very upset. Under questioning she revealed that she had once discovered her husband torturing a cat. Another time he had punished his small son so severely that she and the servants had had to protect the boy from serious injury. The woman had begun to think that her husband was insane. She told them that the nights the doctor was away from home matched the dates of the Ripper's murders.

Shortly thereafter the doctor was questioned. He admitted that he sometimes suffered from loss of memory. Once he had found blood on his shirt; another time there had been scratches on his face.

The inspector examined the doctor's wardrobe and found a tweed suit and overcoat that matched Lees's precognitive description. With this discovery the doctor himself believed that he was actually the Ripper. He then begged the police to kill him, for "he could not live with the knowledge that he was a monster."

He was declared insane and sent to an asylum. His identity was never revealed. No one knows why. All the general public knew was that on November 8, 1888, the last of the Ripper's murders was committed. As far as the public was concerned Jack the Ripper was never apprehended, his identity never established, the case never officially closed.

Criminologists still dispute the number of victims that Jack the Ripper claimed during the autumn of '88. Most agree that he was responsible for the deaths of at least six women who were murdered and then brutally mutilated.

Lees himself was sworn to secrecy. He never broke his pledge. He left a document describing these events and directed that it be opened upon his death.

But even in this document, which formed the basis for Mr. Archer's report, the Ripper's real name was not revealed.

ON JANUARY 16, 1930, SCOTTY MCLAUCHLAN DISAP-peared. He had told friends that he was selling out to his partner and leaving the small Saskatchewan town of Beechy. He was supposed to be at the railroad depot that evening. He never made it. No one ever knew what happened to him.

Again, from *Crime and the Psychic World*, Fred Archer reports that three years later a mind reader called Professor Gladstone came to town. He was to give a performance that night, December 10, 1932. When he was half way through his show the mind reader suddenly stopped. He turned toward one of the men in the audience and said: "You are thinking about your friend Scotty McLauchlan. He was murdered. Brutally murdered."

The man, Bill Taylor, had indeed been a good friend of Scotty's, and he was thinking about him at that very moment. The people in the audience were astonished.

The next day the McLauchlan case was reopened at the request of Constable Carey of the Canadian Royal Mounted Police. He had witnessed the professor's show and wanted to investigate his claim of murder.

Constable Carey, Jack Woods (another Mountie), and Professor Gladstone traveled from house to house pursuing their investigation. At one homestead a farmer was so surprised by how much the Professor knew about his own life that he admitted to them that Scotty's partner, John Schumacher, had been in a wild rage and had once threatened to kill Scotty.

That night they paid a visit to John Schumacher. Soon after they arrived the Professor said that Scotty's body was buried nearby.

When they questioned Schumacher he repeated the same story he had given three years before: he claimed he had bought out his partner, given him his money, and had never seen him again.

Then Professor Gladstone spoke up: "I'll tell you what happened. Scotty went over to the barn. You followed him and started a quarrel." He went on to describe how the two men fought, how Scotty fell to the ground, and how Schumacher then ". . . struck, and struck, and struck." The professor then claimed that Schumacher had buried Scotty's body near the barn. Schumacher would admit nothing.

The next day the Mounties returned with a digging party. The men began their excavation; the sounds of their shovels ripped through the freezing winter air. After two hours of hard work they had found nothing and were ready to give up.

Just then one of the diggers uncovered a man's sock. They kept going: soon they unearthed an entire skeleton. Pieces of decayed cloth still clung to the bones. The skull had been severely fractured. One of the men recognized Scotty's scarf and mackinaw. Faced with the evidence, Schumacher finally confessed.

IN *The Psychic Feats of Olaf Jonsson* BRAD STEIGER gives a full account of one of the most bizarre cases of psychic detection on record. It took place in Tjornap, Sweden, in March 1952.

A Swedish journalist, Leif Lunde, contacted the well-known psychic, Olaf Jonsson, and told him about the mass murders that had taken place in Tjornap. Thirteen people had been killed, and their homes (along with most of the evidence) had been burned. The police had little to go on.

Journalist Lunde had witnessed several psychic experiments in which Jonsson had taken part. He thought perhaps the psychic would be able to help track down the murderer. He had already spoken to police in Tjornap and they had agreed to bring Jonsson in on the case.

Jonsson had given private séances, had conducted ESP experiments in laboratories, and had directed ships through mine-infested waters; but he had never applied his psychic abilities to police work before.

While he was considering the journalist's proposal, Jonsson began to receive impressions about the case.

"He robs them. He—and it *is* a man—murders, then robs. He does not sexually violate his victims. And he has killed both men and women."

In a few moments he received other visions. He could see flames flickering in a corner of his room. Then he saw a woman lying on a floor. She was

53

holding her stomach and bleeding; she was seriously wounded, but not yet dead. Then Jonsson watched as the flames reached her feet. She burst into flames. Her clothing must have been soaked with a combustible liquid. Her terrified screams reverberated in Jonsson's ears. As a result of experiencing this tragic vision, Jonsson made up his mind: he would go to Tjornap.

Shortly thereafter Jonsson, his sister, Leif Lunde, and Erling Tollefsen, a photographer, drove to Tjornap. They were escorted to the various murder sites by a young policeman, Officer Hedin.

In the ruins of one of the victim's homes Jonsson received impressions of "blood and pain but not the murderer's face." Officer Hedin kept asking question after question. Jonsson kept replying that the visions he was seeing were too faint to be of help.

That night everyone dined together. After dinner Officer Hedin left to meet his girl friend. When he was gone Lunde turned to Jonsson and said: "What an earnest and cooperative young officer! He stands there so patiently while you soak up the impressions of each site, Olaf. He will be of great help to you...."

"Yes. He will be of great assistance," the psychic replied.

During the next few days the group completed their tour of the murder sites. At one point Officer Hedin gave Jonsson the remains of a rifle that had been recovered from the house of a female victim. Friends of the woman knew that it didn't belong to her. It was possible that it was the murderer's weapon. Jonsson held the rifle in his hands. After a while he said that he wanted to return to his hotel.

"Did you see the murderer? Can you tell us anything about him?" asked the journalist. Officer Hedin also wanted to know and said: "Tell us what you saw."

Jonsson replied that he just wanted and needed to rest. He hadn't seen a thing, he told them.

He was taken back to his room. Once alone he calmed himself, and then psychically revisited each of the thirteen murders. First he saw a young woman sitting quietly in an armchair, reading. There was a knock at the door. She opened the door and, seeing and recognizing her caller, she asked whether it was official business. Then she saw the rifle.

There was a woman preparing her family's evening meal. The doorbell rang. She went to the door and opened it. The rifle blast ripped through her.

Then a heavy set man was shot in the head.

On and on, murder after murder, and in each there was the same rifle blast, and the same "ice cold eyes sighting along the barrel," the same evil smile. The same face.

When he came out of his room he was calm. He asked his three companions to come inside and lock the door. Everyone gathered around while Jonsson spoke. "The murderer—it is Officer Hedin."

Leif Lunde was shocked. "Are you sure?"

Jonsson replied that he was. He had seen Hedin pulling the trigger the first time he had handed him the charred remains of the rifle. "Of course, I couldn't say anything at the time. If I had, he would have killed us all—I read murder in his mind."

The psychic went on to remind his friends that

55

they were out in the country at the time. No one would have heard a thing. It would have been easy.

"Surely only a madman would have taken such a risk."

Jonsson replied that Hedin *was* mad. Besides, he said, what were another four lives to such a mass murderer who had already taken thirteen? Jonsson now said that they must phone police headquarters and tell them about their helpful young officer.

When Jonsson put the call through he was told that Hedin had disappeared. The next day his body was found. He had committed suicide. In a letter found in his home Officer Hedin confessed to the crimes, and he explained that he had taken his own life because he knew that it was only a matter of time before Jonsson discovered him.

WHEN ENOUGH OF THESE ACCIDENTAL ENCOUNTERS with psychics proved successful, people began to wonder if it was possible to gain some measure of permanent control over the psychic process. Could psychic awareness be consciously and consistently directed toward the solution of crimes?

Unfortunately, existing prejudices against all things psychic made such a long-term collaboration between psychics and police difficult if not impossible.

However, during the last few years attitudes towards ESP have undergone vast revision. Now ESP is not only taken seriously by the general public, but it has been officially recognized by the scientific community as well. This newly won respectability has encouraged police departments across the country to reconsider the possibilities of "psychic assistance." (The CIA and the military have been aware of the possibilities for *many* years.) There is no longer any doubt that psychic abilities can be utilized in crime detection. Nor is there any doubt that police departments have already called upon psychic detectives for help. What remains questionable is the *nature* of their evolving collaboration.

In any case, psychic detection is no longer an accidental affair. Today's psychic detectives are individual psychics who *consciously* and willingly engage in police work. They are all "established" psychics who have gained solid reputations outside of the arena of criminal work before entering the field. Over the years they have been called on time and again to aid police in cases where normal investigation has proven fruitless.

PETER HURKOS

ON JULY 10, 1941, PETER HURKOS, AGED THIRTY, WAS working with his father, helping him paint a four-story building on a street in The Hague. Hurkos placed his tall ladder midway between two windows and climbed up. The job was going smoothly until he reached for the paint bucket, when he lost his balance and fell.

I don't want to die, I want to live! . . . I was falling, I saw my whole life pass before me, and I didn't want to die. . . . I was fighting, fighting. . . .
. . . Then it was black, for a long time black, I am in darkness. . . .
. . . Then there was the light that took me up to the other world, like suction. . . .
. . . Then I see all the colors, I hear the music, I

59

hear the voices and I see the people. . . . I knew I was not dead. . . .

As Norma Lee Browning explains in *Peter Hurkos: I Have Many Lives* and *The Psychic World of Peter Hurkos,* this near death fall marked the beginning of a new life for the Dutch born house painter. When he woke up in the hospital four days later Peter Hurkos had changed.

He looked around him. There was a man in the bed next to his. He had never seen him before, but suddenly he knew a great deal about him. "You're a bad man."

"Why?" the man asked.

"Because when your father died he left you a large gold watch—he died only a short time ago and you have already sold the watch."

In his autobiography, *Psychic,* Hurkos tells us that the man was dumbfounded. He asked Hurkos how he knew about the watch. Hurkos replied that he "just knew it. . . . I was right wasn't I?" The man just nodded with amazement.

A few moments later a nurse came into the room to check Hurkos's pulse. While they were chatting Hurkos suddenly told her that he could see her on a train. He advised her to be careful; she was in danger of losing a suitcase that belonged to a friend of hers. The nurse was startled and dropped his wrist. She had just lost the suitcase that morning. "How did you know?" The nurse had not mentioned it to anyone.

A few days later another patient stepped into the

room to wish Hurkos a speedy recovery. Hurkos recognized the man as someone who had often peeked into his room to see how he was doing. The man was now dressed in his street clothes. He was being discharged from the hospital. He shook hands with Hurkos and said good-bye.

At that moment Hurkos knew that the man was a British agent and that he was going to be killed by the Germans in a few days. The stranger had to struggle to free his hand from Hurkos's frenzied grip. Hurkos found himself unable to speak; he was too astonished by his own vision.

The man finally freed his hand and left the room. Hurkos told the nurse what he had felt about the man. A doctor came into the room to see what the commotion was about. "You must take it easy, Mr. Hurkos, you have a very serious skull fracture . . . you must rest now."

Two days later Hurkos found out that the man had been killed by the Gestapo.

Indeed, something had changed for Peter Hurkos. His accidental fall caused him to become clairvoyant, and it altered the entire course of his life.

Hurkos remembers that time after the fall as being one of intense nervousness and anxiety. Strange visions would pounce on him unexpectedly. He might meet someone for the first time, shake hands, and instantly receive a flood of impressions about their life. Or he might pick up a coin, and if it had been held by someone long enough, it would have a "story" to tell him. Any object could set off the process.

After his release from the hospital Hurkos at

61

first tried to hide from the world. He couldn't stand his "gift" at all. He wanted to stay locked up in his room. But eventually he decided he might as well put his troublesome clairvoyance to work for him. He began giving readings and then performances.

One morning a woman came to see him. She told Hurkos that her husband had disappeared. The police had not been able to locate him. She offered to pay Hurkos anything if he could help her. Hurkos told the woman to return with an object that belonged to her husband.

The woman came back with one of her husband's coats. Hurkos held the coat and then immediately asked about "football" and a "uniform." The woman's husband had indeed been a soccer player. He was now in the army.

The woman became hysterical and started to scream for her husband. Just then Hurkos saw a vision. As Norma Lee Browning reports, Hurkos told the woman what had happened. He could see her husband walk toward the outskirts of town, stop for a moment, then decide to take the shortcut through the woods. He could see the man trip and fall into a tank trap filled with water. The man struggled to free himself but he was too weak because he was drunk. Hurkos then saw the man freezing to death in the water.

"I am sorry, Madame, your husband is dead. . . . Here, I make you a sketch where you find the body." Hurkos then told her to go to the police.

The woman did so. She convinced the police to search the area that Hurkos had described. The police found nothing. The police captain was sure that Hurkos was a fake.

The woman returned to Hurkos and persuaded him to accompany her to the police station. They convinced the police to try again, this time with Hurkos along. After a search they uncovered the dead man's cap and after digging and dredging they found the body.

ON CHRISTMAS DAY, 1950, THE STONE OF SCONE WAS stolen from beneath the coronation chair in Westminster Abbey. Ever since Edward I had brought the Stone to England over six hundred years ago, the English kings and queens had been crowned upon it.

Scotland Yard was at a loss for clues. Many of Hurkos's friends wanted him to travel across the Channel to see if he could help. Letters arrived from people in England. Finally a close friend of Hurkos's who had been in contact with an English man was told that Hurkos would get full cooperation from Scotland Yard. Hurkos decided to go.

He arrived in London and soon after was escorted to Westminster Abbey. Once inside he moved around, trying to get in touch with something that would trigger his psychic visions. He knelt beside the coronation chair and touched it. He began to pick up vibrations. His mind was flooded with images of the history that surrounded the chair; he tried to work through them to get to recent events. After half an hour of trance-like concentration he told the inspectors that five people had been involved. Three had broken in, the others had waited outside in a truck. He described an old church by a river, a bridge, and a cemetery. Then he drew a rough sketch of the area.

The next day he was given the crowbar that the thieves had used to break into the Abbey. He concentrated on it for two hours. By "reading" the crowbar he was able to trace the route the thieves had followed. He asked the police to drive him to Round Pond. When he arrived there he explained that it was the site where the crime had been planned. Later he asked to be taken to a particular street. He got out of the car and walked around to a hardware store. He knew it was the store where the crowbar had been purchased.

Later that day he told the inspectors that the Stone was in Glasgow, Scotland. He explained that it had been stolen by students as a prank. He predicted it would be back in Westminster Abbey within four weeks.

The Stone was later found in the ruins of an old church, Arbroath Abbey, in Scotland. The students who took it admitted that it had been a prank, as Hurkos had said. They had been traced to Glasgow and offered immunity if they returned the Stone in one piece.

In 1956 Peter Hurkos was brought to the United States by Andrija Puharich, M.D., who was the director of the Round Table Foundation in Glen Cove, Maine. The foundation had a well-equipped laboratory designed for psychic research. Hurkos worked with Puharich for two and a half years. When their work was completed Hurkos stayed on in this coun-

64

try, becoming involved with American police departments.

Among the many cases he worked on, perhaps none has been as controversial as the Boston Strangler killings. The Boston Strangler! According to the book and picture of the same name, the person responsible for these ghastly murders was one Albert DeSalvo. After all, DeSalvo confessed to the crimes. Why not take his word?

Peter Hurkos is one man who does not. "DeSalvo is not the killer, and nobody can make me say that he is." According to the police the two hottest suspects in the case were Albert DeSalvo and Thomas P. O'Brien (another suspect's fictitious name). When DeSalvo confessed the investigation was ended.

Hurkos's conviction comes from the six days he spent working on the case. He was called in to help after the Strangler had claimed his eleventh victim, and public outcry had reached a fever pitch.

During Hurkos's first day of work on the case the detectives brought in boxes containing nylon scarves (used by the strangler) and hundreds of photographs of the various crime scenes. The photos were laid face down on the hotel room bed and Hurkos started "feeling" through the stacks. Suddenly he stopped. He picked up one of the pictures and said: "Phony Baloney!" According to Norma Lee Browning, Hurkos went on to say that one of the investigators admitted that he had slipped in a picture from another murder case to test the psychic's ability.

"You want to play tricks, ya. I fly all the way

here to help you and you think Peter Hurkos is a faker? I show you sir!" He went on to tell the officer specific details about each of the stranglings—details that had never been given out to the press. The officers were astonished by Hurkos's descriptions.

In the days that followed, Hurkos went through each of the hundreds of photographs in a desperate search for the killer. It was hard work that was made even more difficult by the all too numerous people constantly surrounding him; he was picking up too many outside vibrations.

At one point Hurkos asked for a map of Boston to be placed upside down before him. Then he asked for an object belonging to one of the victims. One of the detectives handed him a hair comb. He picked it up and moved it over the map. Up and down, back and forth. Then his hand came to rest: "Here . . . here . . . you find the killer. He looks like priest, dresses like priest. . . . He speak French, English. . . . He talk like girl . . . he's pervert. . . ."

The next day Hurkos was given a letter to read that had been received by the Boston College School of Nursing and forwarded to the police. It was from Thomas P. O'Brien, a man who claimed he wanted to meet young nurses for a magazine article he was writing, and for marriage if that proved possible.

Instead of reading the letter Hurkos crumbled it and held it in his hand. ". . . he do it! This the one— he the murderer! Yes, he the man!"

Hurkos went on to describe the suspect. He said he was 5 feet 7 inches (1.45 m) tall, had a mark on his left arm, and something wrong with his thumb. He was a homosexual and a woman hater. He had blue gray eyes and a pointed nose. He said the man killed to offer God a sacrifice. The man also slept in his clothes, and removed the mattress from his bed so he could sleep on the bare springs—his form of self-torture.

Hurkos became so involved in the Strangler Case that he couldn't get the killer out of his mind, not even at night. He would talk to the Strangler in his sleep by assuming two voices, his own and the killer's. In *The Psychic World of Peter Hurkos* Norma Lee Browning quotes Hurkos as explaining that he witnessed most of his visions in his sleep. ". . . I lived through the killings . . . through the mind from that man." One night he took some of the clothing of the victims to bed with him. He then saw the killer's own room and a diary, which he felt would prove to the police that O'Brien was the man they were looking for.

When the police first went to question O'Brien, Hurkos accompanied them. O'Brien wouldn't let them in; he slammed the door in their faces, and he screamed that he didn't want to see anyone. The detectives were astounded. The man had spoken with the same high-pitched voice that Hurkos had adopted in his nightly "conversations" with the Strangler—conversations overheard by these same officers.

The next day the police returned and were accompanied by a doctor. This time O'Brien let them in. He told the detectives that he was glad they had finally come. His person and his room closely matched Hurkos's descriptions. The doctor questioned O'Brien

67

and then signed commitment papers on the spot. O'Brien was taken to the Massachusetts Mental Health Center.

Hurkos then entered the apartment to help with the search. A diary was found with entries that showed that many of Hurkos's impressions had been correct. O'Brien had tried to become a monk, admitted abnormal sexual impulses, and explained that he thanked "you my Lord that I sleep on a steel mattress. . . ."

Later O'Brien was questioned by the police and confronted by Hurkos. He was shown pictures of the murder victims. Hurkos told him that he had done a very bad thing. O'Brien replied: "Yes. I must have done a very bad thing, a very bad thing. But I don't remember it."

O'Brien was questioned repeatedly, but each time he got to the point of admitting that he had actually committed the murders, he always said that he couldn't remember any more. When a doctor questioned him about his mattress, O'Brien said that he didn't want to go back to his room. He thought he should stay in the hospital. That is precisely where he stayed. He was never charged with the crimes.

In fact, no one has ever been formally charged with the stranglings, not even DeSalvo, the man who confessed to them a month after Hurkos left the case.

With DeSalvo's sensational confession all previous suspects were dropped, until four years later when the case was supposed to be reopened with new information that DeSalvo was *not* the strangler. But before anything happened the case was mysteriously dropped for the last time. Apparently DeSalvo's doctors decided that he wasn't fit to take lie detector tests, and therefore further questioning was pointless.

Was Hurkos right? Was O'Brien the real Strangler?

GERARD CROISET

ON MAY 4, 1976, GERARD CROISET WAS WAITING TO appear on a Japanese television program about the occult. Croiset was invited to take part in the program because of his reputation in helping police solve difficult murders and missing persons crimes.

Before rehearsals began for his appearance Croiset stepped into a nearby studio. A man, Takesi Kikuchi, was asking for help in finding his seven-year-old daughter, Miwa. The girl had been missing for over a week.

As reported in the *National Enquirer* (July 20, 1976), the Japanese producer, Haruhiko Matsumura, translated the man's appeal for Croiset. The clairvoyant believed he could help locate the girl. He was given a photograph and a pencil case belonging to Miwa. He began to concentrate.

71

Croiset asked if there was a pond close by the girl's house. A television crew member replied that there was a reservoir about a mile (1.6 km) away. Croiset then asked if there were boats on the water. He was told that there were and that they were secured to a small dock. Then Croiset drew a map of the reservoir and marked the spot where the girl's body would be found.

The following morning a television crew searched the reservoir and discovered the girl's body. It was floating near the dock, as Croiset had described.

Susumu Kagimoto, a director, was the man who first came upon the body. "I just cannot describe my feelings. It seemed completely unreal. . . . This was somebody's daughter floating dead on the water, and we'd found her through the incredible gift of telepathy [actually, clairvoyance] of a foreigner who had never set foot here in all his life."

The police were informed and they notified the child's parents, who later identified the body.

Though remarkable, this clairvoyant performance is by no means rare for Gerard Croiset. He seems to be particularly skilled at locating missing children, especially those that are drowning cases. Perhaps this is a result of his own near drowning when he was eight years old. (Some parapsychologists feel that psychics are most successful when dealing with events that are familiar to their own life experiences.)

Back in Croiset's native Holland, in 1962, a small boy vanished from the town of Slikkerveer. According to Richard Trubo in his *Psychic Magazine* article entitled "Psychics and the Police," when Croiset was contacted he told police that the boy would be found near a large bridge. Unfortunately there was no bridge in the neighborhood. The police ignored Croiset's vision.

Later, while examining blueprints of the vicinity, one of the officers noticed that a bridge was in the *planning* stages. A police squad was sent out to explore the site and the boy was found. He was alive and well.

One of the peculiarities of Croiset's methods is that he often works by telephone. Many of the cases he has been involved with began and ended in his own living room. Croiset believes that the telephone effectively screens out confusing vibrations and helps him focus on the person or problem at hand.

In *Croiset the Clairvoyant* Jackson H. Pollack relates that on December 12, 1959, Croiset received a call from Professor Walter Sandelius, who was a political scientist, a department head, a Rhodes Scholar, and a member of the governor's commission to revise the Kansas Constitution. Professor Sandelius explained that his daughter had disappeared from a hospital where she had been admitted following a nervous breakdown. She had been missing for over a month and the police had not been able to locate her. Could he help? From almost 5,000 miles (8,047 km) away came the reply.

Croiset could see the girl, he knew she was still alive. He described the route she had taken when she left the hospital. He then said she was near a large body of water, with many small boats nearby. He mentioned that he saw her riding there in a truck and a big red car.

Croiset assured Sandelius that there was nothing

to worry about. He told the Professor that he would hear from his daughter after six days. Croiset asked for a photograph of the girl and road maps of the area. It was arranged that Croiset and Sandelius would talk again in six days.

Six days later Sandelius was about to call Croiset as arranged. At 8:00 A.M. he came downstairs. There, sitting on the living room couch, was his daughter. He immediately phoned Holland with the remarkable news.

Later Professor Sandelius found out that his daughter had indeed hitched a ride in a big red car, and then she had gotten a ride with an elderly couple who worked in a carnival. On the day of the first phone conversation with Croiset she had been in Corpus Christi, on the Gulf of Mexico.

BY THE TIME CROISET WAS SIX YEARS OLD HE KNEW he was "different." He realized he could "see" things that other people could not. He felt "set apart" from others and very insecure. People thought him a strange child and avoided him. He was often reprimanded when he spoke out to tell about his psychic impressions. He spent his childhood moving from one foster home to another, and, as a result, his elementary education was disrupted.

Because the young Croiset insisted that he could see things that were happening many miles away, one of his teachers thought he was a "crazy little fool," until Croiset explained why the teacher had missed school the day before. "You went to see a young blond woman who was wearing a red dress with a red rose. You are going to marry her." That was exactly what had happened.

In 1935 the newly married Croiset opened a grocery store with backing from his in-laws. The store soon folded—it was an event he could not foretell about his own life—and he suffered a nervous breakdown.

Soon after Croiset became involved with a group of spiritualists and acted as a medium for the séances that they conducted. At first Croiset felt he belonged, but he soon came to believe that something other than spirits were at work inside him. He left the group.

One day, while visiting the watchmaker Henk de Mar, Croiset picked up a meter stick. Instantly he received impressions about the man's life. "I see an automobile accident . . . a body lying on the road in a grassy place." De Mar replied that everything Croiset had told him was true. When Croiset explained that he had these feelings quite frequently, the watchmaker explained that he must be clairvoyant.

"That's how it all began. Other people heard about me and brought their troubles to me. I forgot about my grocery store failure and started to think of a new career."

That career has been a long and successful one. Croiset has helped the parents of scores of missing children, and he has worked with the police departments in countries all across the globe.

Although he has a reputation for finding missing persons, his case load has not been limited to this kind of work. He has also been involved with murder

75

and sex crimes. Many of these were documented and analyzed by Professor Willem Tenhaeff, a Dutch parapsychologist, and Director of the Parapsychology Institute at the University of Utrecht.

According to Jackson Pollack, on February 4, 1954, Mr. Peter S. S. Guok contacted Croiset. A friend of his had been murdered and he wanted Croiset's help. Professor Tenhaeff supervised a meeting at the institute. The lawyer did not provide any information about the case, nor did he indicate whether Croiset's impressions were accurate.

The experiment was started when Croiset was handed a photograph of the victim. He knew immediately that the man was dead. *"How* did he die?" Croiset wanted to know. Mr. Pollack supplied the description of the scene.

Croiset received impressions of a city that was under a British protectorate, he thought it was Malacca. (The city was actually Singapore.) He felt himself being struck a fatal blow to the head; he saw himself lying on his back with his mouth open.

Croiset said that the murder had something to do with politics. The man had gotten in the way of a particular group and had to be eliminated. (This was correct.)

Next Croiset described a Chinese man, about fifty-four to fifty-six years old, the owner of a store, and a Chinese spy. This man had hired a tall, half-blood Chinese as the hit man. The murdered man did not want to live up to agreements he had made with the group. He was killed to prevent him from betraying the group to the English. (This was confirmed.)

Croiset then provided a description of the area around the suspect's shop. It was very accurate, as the Chinese lawyer later confirmed to Professor Tenhaeff.

Unfortunately, although the Singapore police were astounded by Croiset's "parapsychological bull's-eye," they were unable to arrest the suspect. Hard evidence was lacking. He was later picked up on another charge.

Again, from Pollack's *Croiset the Clairvoyant*, we learn that in June 1958 Croiset was asked to "read" a pair of red slippers. They had been brought from America by a man who did not know their significance. He was doing a favor for an American police official. "If Croiset is so smart . . . see if he can tell me anything about these slippers."

After handling the slippers Croiset explained that they had belonged to a pretty young woman. "She was murdered in her home outside a big city in America near a body of water, by a bushy-haired man."

The slippers belonged to Marilyn Sheppard. She had been murdered four years earlier, July 4, 1954, in her home in Bay Village, Ohio, on Lake Erie. Her husband, Dr. Sam Sheppard, had been sent to jail for the crime; he was not bushy-haired.

During his trial Dr. Sheppard claimed that a "bushy-haired" intruder had killed his wife and knocked him unconscious. Two witnesses at the trial claimed that they saw a bushy-haired man hanging around the Sheppard's home at the time the murder was committed.

Mr. Pollack comments that Dr. Sheppard never

77

changed his story in eleven years. Apparently Croiset supported him: "The red slippers, yes. The bushy-haired man did it—not her husband! I am absolutely sure."

In addition to working for police departments the world over, Croiset has also offered his services to our own FBI. Mr. Pollack explains that on June 27, 1964, he was contacted by a Mr. Milton A. Nelson. A friend of Nelson's on the New York City Police force had suggested that he contact Croiset. He wanted to know if Pollack could arrange things for him. He added that he had spoken to U.S. Representative Ogden Reid, who had agreed to pass Croiset's information on to the attorney general's office in Washington, D.C.

Milton Nelson was a longtime family friend of the Schwerners. Their son Michael, along with James Chaney and Andrew Goodman, had been missing for six days. The three young civil rights workers had disappeared in Mississippi. At that time the FBI and police had no clues to the whereabouts of the missing men.

No one knew whether they were dead or alive. Lawrence Rainey, the sheriff of Neshoba County, Mississippi, explained that if the young men were still in the state, they were probably just hiding out, trying to get publicity. "They've never been bothered here," he said. A search by state troopers and the FBI came up empty-handed.

Pollack put through a trans-Atlantic call to Croiset's home. Soon after the conversation had begun,

Croiset told him that the three boys were dead. He could see it clearly.

He told Pollack that the bodies would be found 15 to 20 miles (24 to 32 km) from the location of their car, in a swampy place, close to construction. (The bodies of the three young men were uncovered on August 4, buried in an earthen dam, 20 miles [32 km] from their charred station wagon.)

These details were forwarded to the FBI, which then requested more information. Croiset complied. Further work on the case revealed that the leader of the murderers was a member of a secret society. He was the son of the owner of a big plantation. He had a war decoration.

Croiset described the general location of the site at which the bodies would be found and the room in which the crime was plotted; he also provided information about the blunt instrument that was used to beat the young black man, James Chaney, before he was shot. Croiset also had the impression that police officers were among the band of conspirators.

Mr. Pollack explains that it is impossible to determine precisely how helpful Croiset's information was to the FBI. The FBI, he says, will not officially admit that it was aided by a psychic. The use of psychics is unofficial. But Pollack insists that Croiset's information must have been of *some* help; "otherwise, why did . . . [they] keep requesting additional information?"

79

IRENE HUGHES

AUGUST, 10, 1966, WAS A HOT AND STICKY NIGHT, but Irene Hughes sat hunched over as if she were freezing. The group of men and women that stood around her in silent disbelief were sweating heavily.

"I s-see s-snow falling. . . . The snow keeps coming down. The flakes are big and white and they just won't stop coming. And . . . there is a terrible wind. It blows death before it." She was shivering, her teeth chattered, she rubbed her hands to keep warm.

After a few minutes, the Chicago psychic whispered that the snow had finally stopped. She now saw a ticker tape. It said January 26, 27, 28, 29.

81

The incident was reported in Brad Steiger's *Know the Future Today*. As Mr. Steiger comments, five months later the city of Chicago was hit by a terrible blizzard. The snow began to fall on January 26, as Mrs. Hughes had predicted. The blizzard lasted four days. *Community Publications*, a local newspaper, received quite a bit of publicity. It was the only paper to have carried Mrs. Hughes's predictions.

Weather forecasters are not the only people who have been impressed with the ESP abilities of Irene F. Hughes. In addition to predicting the weather and national and international events, Mrs. Hughes has gained a solid reputation as a psychic sleuth, and, with it, the respect of many police departments across the country. She has been credited with helping to solve more than fifteen murders for the Illinois police alone.

Like so many other psychic detectives, Mrs. Hughes relies mainly on the technique of psychometry to trigger clairvoyant impressions. "I do psychometry, I hold personal objects . . . through that means, pictures flash through my fingertips to my brain, indicating names and places and situations to me."

In answer to written interview questions, Mrs. Hughes described her first involvement with police work:

I was called into the police station by a chief of police who wanted me to work on a baffling murder case. When I went to the police station he had on his desk a copy of an article that had appeared in the local *Tribune* about . . . my work. He was a very rough type of individual and indicated that he didn't particularly believe in ESP but was willing to try. . . . He took me into another room . . . and he talked with me about the case. Then he got out one of the objects being held for evidence in the case. . . . It happened to be a woman's head! The hair was still on the skull and the blood had matted in the hair.

As I held the head and meditated the name of the woman came out and he was astounded. Then I told him the name of the man who had committed the murder. . . . He told me that they had picked up an individual by that name and were holding him. . . .

I told him that the man had killed four other women and that they would be found. [He] . . . told me he didn't think so, that only one had been killed.

Nevertheless, he assigned me to work for his Sergeant for six months. . . . My information led to them uncovering the murder and finding the four other bodies!

I also sat in the courtroom, holding a personal object belonging to the murderer and indicating when he was lying. . . . I also indicated when his so-called wife was lying and gave dates and times when she was in other places. They wrote it down . . . checked it out and found it to be absolutely accurate.

According to *National Enquirer* reporter Alan Markfield, in 1964 an eighteen-year-old girl disappeared from her Chicago home. She went out for an evening stroll and never returned.

Mrs. Hughes was consulted. The police brought some of the young girl's clothes for the psychic to work with. In a three hour session Mrs. Hughes learned that the girl had been killed. She went on to reenact the murder for the police.

She described the murder weapon as something heavy, such as a brick. She also said that the girl's body would be found near her home, under a tree. Next she told the investigators the name and address of the murderer. (This is quite rare. Most often psychics receive general impressions, an overall physical description, for example.) Finally she predicted that the case would take a very long time to solve.

It took almost three years for the murderer to be apprehended. Although he had indeed lived at the address provided by Mrs. Hughes, he had evaded capture by being constantly on the move. He never stayed in one place for more then a few days, traveling from city to city across the country.

As Paul Tabouri explains in *Crime and the Occult,* there is a plaque on the wall of Mrs. Hughes's office bearing witness to the aid she provided with this case; on it can be seen the signatures of three policemen.

In March 1970 the Chicago police were busily dredging a South Side canal. They were trying to locate the body of a shooting victim, but their efforts were unsuccessful. Mrs. Hughes was consulted. "I asked a detective where they had been looking and he said 'over to the left.' I said, 'No wonder you didn't find him. The body's way over there under some rocks.' "

She went on to say that "the body was coatless

and one shoe was missing, and the man was in a white shirt." The next morning a passerby discovered the body in the general area that Mrs. Hughes had described.

Virgil Jordan, assistant police chief of Kankakee, Illinois, has requested Mrs. Hughes's help on several different occasions. One case involved the killing of a fellow police officer. Although the entire department had been working overtime for several weeks, they had still not found the killer.

Assistant police chief Jordan brought a stack of photographs to Mrs. Hughes and placed them on a table. Mrs. Hughes said that the killer wasn't among them. Then another group of photographs was placed before her. *National Enquirer* reporter Alan Markfield quotes Jordan's description of what happened next. ". . . . She said the man who did it was in that group but it was an old photo of him. She said he was a short, dark man who often wore an army fatigue hat backwards. That description matched exactly a suspect we had in custody." The man in the fatigue hat later confessed to the crime and was convicted.

According to Paul Tabouri, Mrs. Hughes was also involved in the search for the kidnapped British diplomat James Cross, and the Quebec Cabinet Minister Pierre La Porte. In the fall of 1970 she was interviewed by a Canadian broadcaster. She predicted that La Porte would be harmed, Cross would be safe. This is precisely what happened. Cross was later released. La Porte was found dead in the trunk of a car.

THIS IS THE SAME IRENE HUGHES, WHO, AT AGE FOUR, explained to her mother that she had just passed part of the afternoon up in the attic talking to a "fairy queen" and a "little man." Irene had always known that these little people lived nearby, she could feel their presence. This was the first time she had seen them. They had promised the little girl a present of beads and a doll.

Most parents would have smiled, laughed, or tried to smack some sense into their child. But Irene's mother was used to hearing fantastic stories from the mouth of her little daughter—stories that often became realities.

According to Brad Steiger these are Mrs. Hughes's feelings about her unique childhood:

> The thing for which I am most grateful to my mother is her understanding of my power of prophecy. She made me know I was a normal child with a special God-given gift of being able to see what was hidden to others. She never laughed at me or made me feel foolish. She never scolded me or tried to whip the "devil" out of me.

One evening Irene visited an old woman who had worked with the family. The woman was ill and afraid that she was going to die. She wanted to give her little friend a present. She handed Irene a shoe box: inside were two strands of beads. When Irene returned home, two of her sisters' friends were there waiting. They had come to give Irene an old doll that they had outgrown.

Irene's life seemed to be filled with such incidents. Brad Steiger describes one that occurred when Irene was fifteen years old. She was walking home from church one night when she suddenly heard a voice scream out, "Irene, get on the tracks! Get on the streetcar tracks!" Without thinking, she obeyed.

She stood absolutely still between the rails and waited. Just then a car came down the road. As it approached, its headlights illuminated a large snake, coiled and ready to strike.

If she had not obeyed the voice she would have walked right into its fangs. Still, she was not completely out of danger. She was just barely out of reach of its striking range.

The driver of the car then saw the snake. He turned the steering wheel toward it and crushed it.

Where had the voice come from? Who had saved her? There was no one on the street.

Mrs. Hughes believes that whatever warned her was the same natural survival mechanism that is triggered in most people in times of danger. But the difference between Mrs. Hughes and us is that most of us have become so "civilized" that we no longer are able to pay attention to these private alarm systems of ours. Mrs. Hughes points to the examples of the Australian aborigines who, anthropologists claim, can "sense" the presence of danger, as well as to her belief that primitive men could do the same.

For herself, Mrs. Hughes has accepted the presence of this inner survival mechanism and knows that she will always be protected.

ON THAT SAME HOT AUGUST NIGHT THAT MRS. Hughes accurately predicted the great blizzard of '67, she also took a psychic trip *backward* in time. The event was to commemorate the Chatsworth, Illinois, train disaster that had taken place eighty years earlier, on August 10, 1887.

A railroad trestle had caught fire that night. The onrushing train could not be stopped in time and it plunged into the gorge.

Mrs. Hughes was handed two old splintered boards. As soon as her fingers touched the weathered wood they began to tremble. She could see a train filled with "laughing happy people." Some of the passengers were already asleep, others were holding hands or napping.

Suddenly she saw a frightening vision: two men were down below the trestle. They were setting fire to the beams. Mrs. Hughes cried for help. She pleaded for someone to stop them.

But no one did. She then witnessed the horrible tragedy. She saw men and women frantically trying to put out the fire. They were throwing dirt dug up with bloodied hands. The men who had set the fire were now methodically robbing the dead and the dying.

Did Mrs. Hughes really experience a vision of an

eighty-year-old crime? Skeptics might say that she only picked up, telepathically, the vibrations of rumors that had surrounded the tragedy. Rumors that hinted of just such a bloody plan to fire the bridge and rob the vacationing passengers.

At the moment, there is no way to judge, one way or the other.

BEVERLY JAEGERS

BEVERLY JAEGERS, PRESENTLY OF CREVE COEUR, Missouri, is a third-generation police officer. Her grandfather, father, uncles, brother, and sister-in-law are all involved in law enforcement. Mrs. Jaegers is a licensed private investigator who works with police departments across the country. What sets her apart from the other police persons in her family is the fact that Beverly Jaegers is a *psychic* detective.

Unlike the other psychic detectives we have met, Mrs. Jaegers was not born psychic; she never "became aware" of her abilities as a child, never heard strange voices, never fell off of a ladder and landed on her head. Instead, she trained herself to develop the psychic talents she now possesses.

About ten years ago Mrs. Jaegers became interested in psychic research. She read the various testing procedures being used by American and Russian scientists to determine if someone has ESP. She took these tests and used them as teaching tools to develop these abilities in herself.

The *St. Louis Globe Democrat* carried an article describing some of Mrs. Jaegers's training techniques:

> SKIN SIGHT: Use a hardware store paint selection chart that has been cut into squares, with each colored square mounted on a white card. Placing a card face down in the left palm (unless you are a natural lefty), and allowing airspace between the card and palm, try to familiarize yourself with the feeling of different colors. Then try to guess the colors.
>
> MAILBOX TEST (precognition): Some time before the mail is delivered sit down with a notebook and note impressions of how many envelopes will be delivered and what color and size they will be. When your rate of success improves, try to picture who sent the various letters and what they contain.
>
> NEWSPAPER PRECOGNITION: In a similar manner, relax and ask yourself what the headlines on tomorrow's edition of this newspaper will be. . . .

It takes time and work before you begin to see results. You have to be willing to apply yourself. Mrs. Jaegers cautions that the experimenter should be willing to work seriously and to spend several hours a day for at least a week or two if he or she wants to get noticeable results.

For herself, Mrs. Jaegers wanted more then mere

noticeable results. She trained for months. Eventually her abilities began to develop.

In answer to written interview questions, Mrs. Jaegers comments on her procedures:

> ... Through continuous practice ... [I] was able to develop the abilities in myself. Precognition, psychometry, clairvoyance, telepathy. In that sense, I am a true pioneer. No one here in America was doing that at that time, many are still not aware that it can be done. ... Family and friends wanted to know why I was doing it. ... My father, a cop, thought I was trying to be some kind of fortune teller. He is now, however, my biggest supporter. ...

Mrs. Jaegers believes that anyone can learn to develop their own ESP abilities. "Psychic abilities are something we all have and can . . . develop. They are not 'gifts' and they are not 'powers.' That word 'power' has done more to discredit the field of ESP research then any other. People translate that into 'power over me' and are scared of it."

Mrs. Jaegers has taught many people to mobilize their latent psychic talents. Several years ago she began a psychic rescue squad to help people "who had gotten into trouble with the occult or witchcraft or spiritualism." Later the group changed its focus to criminal investigation. It has since become a licensed detective agency (in St. Louis, Missouri) and is now called the United States PSI Squad.

The headquarters branch has over twenty members, all of whom have been trained by Mrs. Jaegers.

The men and women who make up this remarkable group come from all walks of life. There is a real estate salesperson, an attorney, a teacher, a pilot, an astrological researcher, a police detective, a housewife, a microbiologist, and a freelance writer.

In addition there are branches of the squad in Texas, California, New York, Maryland, Florida, and Louisiana. According to Paul Tabouri, Mrs. Jaegers's goal is to organize a "chain of psychics" who will be ready to help when and where they are needed. The members of each local branch would be "put on the 'scent.' "

Mrs. Jaegers explains how the group works. "We have all learned to do our work in a completely awake and aware state, no trances, no séances . . . both halves of the mind are operating, conscious and subconscious." They receive an object from the police department they are working with: "a bullet, clothing, ropes which have been used to tie the victim, crime scene photographs of many types—photos of victims before and after."

The members of the group simply hold the object in their left hands and write down their impressions with their right hands. "Squad members can be sitting side by side and working on three or four cases . . . When we are finished we might make a tape recording, each squad member reading into the tape what his findings were." The impressions that squad members receive might not make any sense to them, but they are all recorded for police analysis.

The case that brought Mrs. Jaegers public attention involved the mysterious disappearance of a St. Louis housewife. Mrs. Sally Lucas had been on her way to a Florida vacation: she never arrived there. Anthony Damico was later picked up in her car. The police charged him with murder. At that time the body had not yet been discovered.

The day before Damico was arrested the police presented Mrs. Jaegers with a powder puff and a nightgown belonging to Sally Lucas. Later, when the car was recovered, she sat at the wheel to see if she could pick up impressions about the crime.

The *St. Louis Globe Democrat* of September 6, 1971, carried the story. (It was later reenacted for an NBC documentary about psychic detectives.)

The following are some of Mrs. Jaegers's impressions recorded the day before the body was found:

> Pain, right side of the head and neck, a feeling almost like a cut, impression of a small person, medium length hair, not a heavy smoker, female.

When Mrs. Lucas's body was examined, it was discovered that the blow that killed her landed on the right side of her head. She was a moderate smoker, she was 5 feet (1.52 m) tall, and she had medium length hair.

> Impression of men in uniform bending over looking into a car, near water. . . . I have the feeling she will not be found alive. . . . my deepest impressions are that the woman will be found in or near water.

95

When Mrs. Jaegers sat in the murdered woman's car, she was able to provide further psychic details. "Head hurt—hit water again—man dragging a body. Time, near 4:47 . . . Bridge is very near." (Eventually the body was discovered 50 yards [46 m] from a small bridge.)

Mrs. Jaegers also received impressions about the numbers 3 and 4. These numbers were part of the license plate of Sally Lucas's car. She was also thought to have vanished between 3:00 and 4:00 P.M.

In addition, Mrs. Jaegers "saw" an airplane, the letter C, a horse and a horse's head. The body was discovered near the Spirit of St. Louis Airport, near highways C and CC, just off Wild Horse Creek Road.

With regard to the murderer himself Mrs. Jaegers said that he was

> someone who boasts about his plans and takes credit for things he hasn't done. . . . This was not a robbery—the motive was sexual but twisted. . . . An infantile mind. . . . he loves the night.

On another case Mrs. Jaegers experienced a precognitive vision. She predicted the death of a kidnapped child. "[We] . . . tried very hard to get to him before he was killed . . . but because of legal red tape, was not able to get a search warrant and he was found several days later . . . how I had predicted, and dead only eight hours."

As it was reported in the *National Enquirer* (October 4, 1973), a St. Louis juvenile officer, Charles Kirkwood, said he asked Mrs. Jaegers for help in tracing the body of a six-year-old boy who police believed had been murdered. "Bevy's information was accurate. She led me right near a vacant building where we eventually found the boy's body."

The same article described another case that the PSI Squad worked on. It was a suicide. Detective Joe Messina said Mrs. Jaegers's findings were exactly like his own. This feeling was echoed by Detective Franklin D. Harris. "The victims in a burglary case I was working on asked the squad for help. We had no objections and, as it worked out, the squad's findings coincided with mine." Detective Milton Shepp added: "Bevy has a gift. I have a lot of faith in her. I took a case involving a con artist and large sums of money. She came through with accurate information for me."

Mrs. Jaegers explains that her Psychic Squad *only* works on police cases, that her group does not like to discuss their work, and that their work is "classified."

In addition to police work the PSI Squad has also been involved with archeological investigations. Members have taken part in experiments designed to reconstruct events and situations that happened long ago. One such experiment was reported in the *National Enquirer* on September 8, 1974.

Professor James Radford sent the PSI Squad a single tooth from a skull unearthed at a Mississippi Indian burial site. Eight members of the squad took

97

part in the experiment. Each handled the tooth and recorded their impressions. They reported that the tooth had come from a mass burial site in a thick, misty forest. The tooth had come from a male and was five hundred to one thousand years old. They also felt that the ancient man "had cultivated crops, relied on river travel and used clam shells for tools." Finally they added that he had received a skull wound.

Professor Radford declared their report astounding. "The tooth was just a simple tooth. It would have been impossible to tell offhand if it came from someone who was dead ten or ten thousand years. And I'm convinced that no one in the group had any archeological training at all."

According to Professor Radford the tooth was eight hundred years old, came from a male, and, most impressively, the skull from which it came had indeed suffered a wound.

Mrs. Jaegers has strong feelings about parapsychological research. She says she has no interest in being "tested," that her work stands as her proof.

"American parapsychology is still enmeshed in 'is ESP true?' rather than the pragmatic thrust of Soviet parapsychology which says 'What can it do— let's look'. . . . Their attitude is more realistic than ours has been." She adds that the "cautious tip-toeing done in most labs" has held back the development of psychic technology.

Because of her philosophical beliefs and her conviction that ESP can be taught, Mrs. Jaegers has been called the "mechanic of ESP." The *St. Louis Globe*

Democrat (of August 7 and 8, 1976) quotes her as saying: "A mechanic. Taking it apart to understand it and putting it back together again. I guess that's what I am. I take it as the ultimate compliment."

PSYCHICS AND THE POLICE

IF YOU WERE THE CHIEF INSPECTOR ON A DIFFICULT homicide investigation, would you welcome the help of a psychic detective?

After having explored the world of ESP, seen how ESP has been used by other cultures, and met some of our most famous psychic detectives, you would probably answer yes to the above question. Perhaps you would be enthusiastic about working with a psychic detective. After all, you might wonder, wouldn't *every* police official be happy to take advantage of the benefits of psychic detection?

Unfortunately the answer is no. Not all police departments are open-minded about the possibilities of psychic detection. In fact, psychic detection is still a highly controversial field. There are those who believe in it and those who do not.

Sometimes police officials have been reluctant to work with psychic detectives who are also psychic entertainers (like Peter Hurkos). Perhaps they fear that the psychic is only interested in creating publicity for his or her act. Perhaps they feel that the psychic detectives have greatly exaggerated the worth of their own work in criminal cases.

Other police officials may be threatened by the strangeness of the whole concept of psychic detection, or fear an onslaught of adverse publicity in the press for being forced to rely on such an unorthodox technique. Still others might be annoyed by the prospect of a lone civilian coming up with the solution to a case that they themselves couldn't solve with all their experience and modern police methods.

Among police departments that have used psychics some have claimed success, while others have come away skeptical of the whole affair. Some have been convinced that psychic detectives are phony, while others have been impressed with their psychic abilities, whether or not the psychic detective was able to help solve their particular case.

Then, too, the solution of serious criminal cases is often a complicated affair, even when a psychic detective is on the case. It is not simply a matter of handing a photograph to a psychic detective and then sitting back and letting him or her solve the case for you. Only rarely does a psychic come up with the specific name and address of the criminal.

Most often the psychic's impressions provide

more general descriptions—a physical description of a burglar that might apply to many men, or the description of a building that could be one of many in a large city. At other times the psychic's perceptions can be vague, or he or she may provide specific information that no one is able to decipher.

Often, before sense can be made of the psychic's visions, the police have to investigate the case thoroughly and develop a complete workup on the background of the case. The police can then take the leads provided by the psychic, render them usable, then follow these leads in their own investigation. Remember, the police still need to uncover hard evidence— a confession, fingerprints, stolen merchandise, a body —before they can take their case to court.

Psychic detection has a long way to go before it is perfected as a crimefighting tool and integrated with the overall law enforcement network.

In "The Police and Psychics" (*Psychic Magazine,* May/June 1975) Richard Guarino explained that he had read many accounts from "psychics" who claimed to have helped police, but that he "had not read any statements by police officers that this was so."

In order to satisfy his curiosity, he sent questionnaires to one hundred of the largest city police departments in the country. (His survey was limited: no county police or federal law enforcement agencies were questioned.) Sixty-eight police departments returned the forms. Seven replied that they had used psychics. Sixty-one said they never had.

The Honolulu police claimed that they had worked

with psychics only twice in the last twenty years. On these occasions the *families* of missing persons requested the psychic's help. The psychic was given no official recognition by the police. The Honolulu police claimed that no information of value was provided by a psychic in any case.

The San Francisco police replied that intuition and hunches did play an important part in their work, but that they never found it necessary to try clairvoyance. They further stated their belief that the impressions supplied by psychics were normally based upon information that had already been published. They were not only skeptical of the "psychic's ability to aid police departments *but also in the ability of psychics to obtain information from any manner other than the five senses."* [My italics.]

The New York City Police Department reported that they had used psychics on many occasions. But, as Mr. Guarino explains, no "substantial results" were ever derived from their investigations. They also said that in some cases investigations were slowed down by the pursuit of false leads provided by the psychics.

According to the survey four unnamed police departments had worked on homicides with Peter Hurkos. Each claimed that the evidence supplied by Hurkos was not helpful in solving the cases.

In one instance Hurkos came up with the description of the killer and his hangouts and a list of possible names. The detective who worked with him said he believed that Hurkos was completely sincere, that Hurkos did things that were difficult to explain logically. However, Mr. Guarino states that his information didn't help solve the case.

Unfortunately, Mr. Guarino's survey does not account for unofficial cases of cooperation between psychics and police. As he himself points out, there is no way to determine the extent to which individual detectives have gone to psychics for help. For example, the Los Angeles Police Department reported that although they never *officially* recognized psychic findings, there were "rare occasions only" when individual detectives had considered the impressions provided by "so-called psychics," *unofficially*.

Despite this admission Mr. Guarino goes on to conclude that "the information provided by psychics has not been of help in solving police cases." He continues by saying that "this does not mean that no police department has ever been aided by psychics or that psychics are unable to do so. However, it does indicate that psychics have been used less frequently and with less success than many of us have been led to believe."

There are those who would take issue with this conclusion. According to Beverly Jaegers psychics have probably been used *more* frequently then we have been led to believe.

You would be extremely surprised if you knew just how many police departments work with us, and where they are located. Unfortunately, we cannot mention them. . . . At this time, we are working for a large

105

force here in Missouri, an Attorney General's Office in a western state, and the Major Case Squad in another state (three separate cases, one disappearance, two homicides), a total of seven active files. . . .

We are viewed very well by police officials. We accept *only* police referrals, none from the general public since 1975 or early 1976. We act as consultants to police departments nationally who are faced with unsolvable crimes. . . .

This chaos and controversy, these claims and counterclaims, are not at all unusual for so revolutionary a field as psychic detection. But it does make an accurate appraisal of its efficiency and significance difficult.

Mrs. Jaegers goes on to say that the best way to convince people about the practical uses of psychic abilities is through competent and professional work that is "not couched in terms of mysticism."

Norma Lee Browning, in gathering information for her book *Peter Hurkos, I Have Many Lives,* provides us with another instance of the confusion surrounding police/psychic cooperation. She accompanied Hurkos on several criminal cases, one of which was the Tate/LaBianca murders.

In her notebook she recorded the fact that after two weeks, Hurkos was suddenly dropped from the case and warned to keep his "hands off!" It was a total about-face from the cooperation he had been getting from the Los Angeles Police until that time. It also seemed to contradict the fact that the chief of police was supposedly impressed with Hurkos's work and was following up the leads the psychic had provided.

Irene Hughes explains that part of the reason for the general public's ignorance of the work of psychic detectives is that there is no general police department policy recognizing police/psychic cooperation. Instead, it is "the police officers assigned to a *particular case* [my italics] . . . that contact me and work with me, and often, there is no evidence of their work with me." Mrs. Hughes adds:

> I feel that it varies as to why they do not like to discuss it [their involvement with psychics]. Most of them really believe in it [ESP]. . . . most of them have very intuitive feelings about things themselves, but . . . feel that . . . people in the media would laugh. . . . More than that, perhaps some feel legal complications could arise . . . [in terms of] submitting such evidence in court, or indicating that they had contacted a psychic. I think they try to protect their work. . . .

Beverly Jaegers points out another problem that police have when considering whether or not to accept an offer of help from a psychic. The police are continually bombarded with all manner of offers to help and information from a rather bizarre set of characters. The problem is, how to separate "the nuts from the real psychics."

And then, as Allan Vaughan points out, the police that *do* work with psychics often do not know how to collaborate successfully with them. For example, the police will often tell the psychic everything they know about a particular case. This is the last thing that the psychic needs. It will only confuse things for him. As Mr. Vaughan explains: "The first rule in making effective use of psychics is: don't tell them anything. The less a psychic knows logically, the better the chances for his being able to tap psychic levels."

Mr. Vaughan further explains that police often fail to provide the psychic with a supportive emotional environment. If the police are skeptical and make the psychic feel on trial, they may well inhibit his work.

In an interview in *Psychic Magazine* Peter Hurkos talks about the attitude of police toward his work.

> . . . There is always skepticism when a psychic works with the police—he has to prove that he has the gift . . . unless I convince all those working on the case that I can help, there is little cooperation. . . .

Allan Vaughan continues to explain that better use could be made of psychics if they were contacted as soon as a case breaks, at a time when there are still possible clues and suspects. If they are brought into a case early enough, they could help police determine which suspects to investigate, and where possible evidence might be found. Unfortunately, psychics are too often called upon only when all other police methods fail to produce results.

Mr. Vaughan suggests that when working with psychic detectives, the police should bring personal objects belonging to the victim. After allowing the psychic to handle the objects "a good first question is 'What can you tell me about this person?' If the victim is a young girl and the psychic begins to speak about an old man, then the police don't have to go any further, 'the psychic connection is not being made.'"

If the psychic *does* give an accurate description of the victim, then a second question might be, "'Where is this person now?' The psychic might be able to describe a general location, a house, and other details that might link up with information already known to the ... [police]."

It is important to remember that the psychic's impressions must be measured against facts already known. These impressions cannot be followed blindly. It is very possible for the psychic to pick up information having nothing at all to do with the case in question. Unless these impressions are intelligently evaluated, they can easily lead the police investigators astray. In addition, psychics, like the rest of us, are human: they make mistakes.

In *Beyond Coincidence* Alex Tanous, a Maine psychic, has this to say about mistakes: "In police cases, as with everything I've done, I've had my share of partial successes and total failures. The failures aren't very interesting. I was simply wrong. This does happen—not very often fortunately."

Irene Hughes adds that she too has made mistakes. "Who doesn't. However, I am convinced that the mistakes were due to misinterpretation ... you see the vibrations come from the object—I don't create them ... mistakes can be made through a misunderstanding of the work going on."

Mistakes? Beverly Jaegers says, "I cannot answer that one really. I do not believe we have ever made a real 'mistake' but we have often bombed out on a case and not come in with enough to make our results work for the police. Sometimes there just isn't enough information available . . . we don't know why."

Not every psychic wants to be a crime fighter. Neither does every psychic have the emotional make-up needed to deal with the horrors of rape, murder, and the whims of the criminally insane. In addition, police work carries with it the risk of danger.

In any event, right now the psychic detectives working with police are psychics first and detectives second. Perhaps this is the core of the problem. One way of solving it would be to train the police to be their *own* psychic detectives.

Beverly Jaegers thinks that this is indeed the best solution. She explains that "the answer is not in getting the police to use psychics . . . but . . . in the training of police to use their own innate psychic abilities to work on their own cases." Mrs. Jaegers is currently preparing a training program for the "Major Case Squad of a large western state," which is intended to be a "pilot" program for police all over the United States.

Allan Vaughan suggests that, in addition to learning karate and marksmanship, the police of the future will be trained to master their own clairvoyant, precognitive, and telepathic powers.

CONCLUSION

WILL THE POLICE TRAINING OF THE FUTURE INCLUDE psychic instruction? Or is this merely a futuristic dream?

Many researchers now believe that psychic abilities are a common characteristic of the human race, one that either lies dormant within us or operates without our awareness. At present they are within the conscious control of a precious few of us—our psychics.

But the study of psychic phenomena is still in its infancy. It is quite possible that the pursuit of current lines of research will uncover the precise nature of the psychic process and explain exactly what it is and how it works. Once we understand the nature of the process, we may be able to develop techniques

111

for gaining control of it. Once control is established, we can put these psychic abilities to work for us, direct them as we please.

What are the chances of tapping these psychic resources? According to Stanford Research Institute futurologist Duane Elgin the chances are good. Elgin believes that "some 20 percent of the American population will be practicing psychics by the mid-1980s." * Elgin admits that this is only a "ballpark figure," but then adds, "Look, what if only 1 percent of the American population is (becomes) psychic . . . that's more than 2 million people."

Given our new scientific and cultural openness toward psychic phenomena, and given the increasing attention being focused on the problems of their development, we may very well see such dramatic results in the near future.

As widespread control of the psychic process becomes a reality, we will begin developing psychic technologies; like the peoples of more primitive cultures, we will try to find useful roles for our psychic resources to play.

Psychic crime detection is one such technology that is *already* under way. Still in its pioneering stages, it can only become increasingly more sophisticated, efficient, and important as the psychic revolution takes hold.

* From William S. Stuckey, "Psychic Power: The Next Superweapon," *New York Magazine.*

BIBLIOGRAPHY

Archer, Fred. *Crime and the Psychic World.* New York: William Morrow, 1969.

Browning, Norma Lee. *Peter Hurkos: I Have Many Lives.* New York: Doubleday, 1976.

————. *The Psychic World of Peter Hurkos.* New York: Doubleday, 1970.

Capra, Fritjof. *The Tao of Physics.* Berkeley, Calif.: Shambala Pub., 1975.

Castaneda, Carlos. *The Teachings Of Don Juan.* Berkeley, Calif.: University of California Press, 1968; New York: Ballantine Books, 1969.

————. *Tales Of Power.* New York: Simon and Schuster, 1974.

Córdova-Rios, Manuel and Lamb, F. Bruce. *Wizard of the Upper Amazon.* New York: Atheneum, 1971.

Elgin, Duane. "Power of Mind: The Threat and The Promise." *New Realities,* vol. I, no. I, 1977.

Guarino, Richard. "The Police and Psychics." *Psychic,* May/June, 1975.

Holroyd, Stuart. *Psi and The Consciousness Explosion.* New York: Taplinger Pub., 1977.

Hurkos, Peter. *Psychic.* New York: Bobbs Merrill, 1961.

Koestler, Arthur. *The Roots Of Coincidence.* New York: Vintage Books, 1972.

LeShan, Lawrence. *The Medium, The Mystic, And The Physicist.* New York: Ballantine Books, 1975.

Mackenzie, Andrew. *Riddle of the Future.* New York: Taplinger Pub., 1975.

Moss, Dr. Thelma. *The Probability of the Impossible.* Los Angeles: J. P. Tarcher, 1974.

Pollack, Jackson H. *Croiset the Clairvoyant.* New York: Doubleday, 1964.

Psychics. Editors of Psychic Magazine. New York: Harper and Row, 1972.

Puharich, Andrija. *Beyond Telepathy.* New York: Doubleday/Anchor Books, 1973.

Reichbart, Richard. "The Navajo Hand Trembler: The Multiple Roles of the Psychic in Traditional Navajo Society." *Journal of the American Society for Psychical Research*, October, 1976.

Rhine, Louisa E. *Psi: What Is It?* New York: Harper and Row, 1975.

Schwartz, Berthold. *Parent-Child Telepathy*. New York: Garrett Pub., 1971.

Shelton, Russell H. *My Passport Says Clairvoyant*. New York: Hawthorn Press, 1974.

Steiger, Brad. *Know the Future Today*. New York: Warner Paperback Library, 1970.

———. *The Psychic Feats of Olaf Jonsson*. Englewood Cliffs, N.J.: Prentice Hall, 1971.

Stuckey, William K. "Psychic Power: The Next Superweapon?" *New York Magazine*, Dec. 27, 1976/Jan. 3, 1977.

Tabouri, Paul. *Crime and the Occult*. New York: Taplinger Pub., 1974.

Tanous, Alex, with Ardman, Harvey. *Beyond Coincidence*. New York: Doubleday, 1976.

Targ, Russell and Puthoff, Harold. *Mind Reach*. New York: Delacorte Press, 1977.

Trubo, Richard. "Psychics and the Police." *Psychic*, May/June, 1975.

Vaughan, Alan. "Police: How to Use Psychics." *Psychic*, May/June, 1975.

Van De Castle, R. L. "The Cuna Indians of Panama." *Journal of Communications*, Winter 1975.

Van Over, Raymond. *ESP and the Clairvoyants*. New York: Award Books, 1970.

Warren, William. "Is Jim Thompson Alive and Well in Asia?" *New York Times*, 21 April 1968.

Wavell, S., Butt, A., and Epton, N. *Trances*. New York: E. P. Dutton, 1967.

Wilhelm, John L. *The Search For Superman*. New York: Pocket Books, Inc. 1976.

Young, Samuel. *Psychic Children*. New York: Doubleday, 1977.